Demacrash!

By: Robert L. Kelly

Democrats = A Crash! A Demacrash! You can bet on it. The next five years will be perilous for people invested in the financial markets. Fortunes will be made and lost by dramatic price movements in equities, debt, foreign exchange and commodity markets. This book will prepare you to survive and thrive during the onslaught.

But, which way will markets turn? Some will go up---while others go way down---and some will experience gut-wrenching, roller-coaster rides which investors have never seen before.

The stakes are sky high. The White House, along with control of the House of Representatives and U.S. Senate, are within the grasp of the Democrats. Will they take control? Will they use the markets to attain victory?

Get ready America. Get ready World. The Debt Apocalypse is approaching---dead ahead!

A   PUBLICATION

JACKASS BANKER™

Debt Apocalypse!

47,000 ? 5?

37,000 ? 5?

DEMACRASH !

27,398.68
DJIA High
July 16, 2019

27,719.00
Fake-Out High?

Trump Counter-Punch
Greatest Bull Market Ever

Commodity Storm!
Inflation & Fast-Rising
Interest Rates!

3.

Zig-Zag
Set Up

DEMACRASH

4?

9,900?

Dow Jones Industrial Average 1998-2032
Trump Victory Forecast

© 2019 Robert L. Kelly
www.jackassbanker.com

2016-01-02 2017-01-02 2018-01-02 2019-01-02 2020-01-02 2021-01-02 2022-01-02 2023-01-02 2024-01-02 2025-01-02 2026-01-02 2027-01-02 2028-01-02 2029-01-02 2030-01-02 2031-01-02 2032-01-02

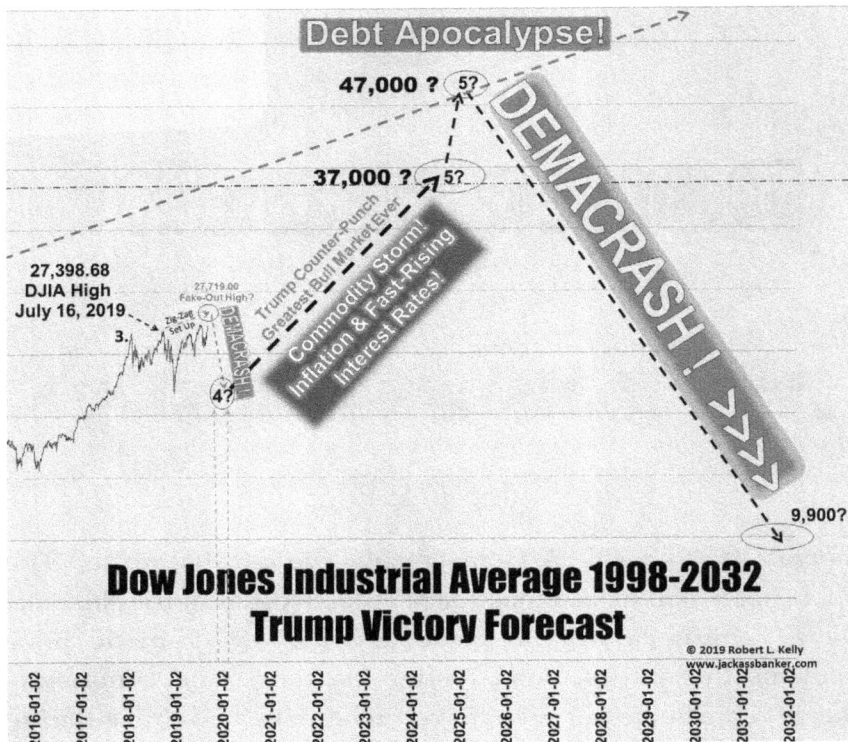

DEMACRASH!
By: Robert L. Kelly

Library of Congress Control Number: 2019950608
All Rights Reserved. New York, New York Printed in the U.S.A.
© 2019 Robert L. Kelly

Jackass Banker™ Publications
412 N. Main Street, Ste. 100
Buffalo, WY 82834

A   PUBLICATION
JACKASS BANKER™

Acknowledgements

I would like to thank the people who have stood by me during the last ten years, as they are my family and loved ones---Heidi, John, Ryan, Tara, Craig, Johnny, David, Michael, Scott, Al, Simon, Dan, Dave, Carl, Willie, Tim, Ed and Mike, along with Vic and his entire clan.

Without them, I don't know where I would be today.

I owe a debt of thanks to everyone---and continue to carry with me the conviction of grace, the certainty of forgiveness, the boldness of preparation---and the humbleness of life which keeps me pressing ahead.

---Love,

Bob/UB/Robert/Dad

Did You Know?

Did you know Robert Kelly has conducted two free, multi-month advanced public educational trading exercises where he traded a million-dollar model portfolio? Trading live in 2018 & 2019, he posted each theoretical trade publicly at the www.jackassbanker.com web site at the time of execution (i.e. all 70 trades in 2019 were "time stamped" with Gmail).

What were the results of these two educational exercises?

They were, indeed, impressive:

- +124% from March 26, 2019 – June 24, 2019
- +84% from April 10, 2018 – June 10, 2018

The figures above are "actual" percentages achieved during the trading time-frames for each educational demonstration. They are not "annualized." While the results used leverage, if the leverage was removed to reflect a traditional, non-leveraged portfolio, the performance was amazing.

If you are trying to manage a pension fund, retirement fund, or are an otherwise sophisticated and qualified investor, take a visit to the Jackass Banker website: http://www.jackassbanker.com/contact-us Jackass Banker engages in structural and economic consulting for corporations and institutions. If you are not properly protected from the upcoming financial storm, give us a call.

Jackass Banker helps companies hedge foreign currency transactions and provides CEOs and CFOs a big edge in the management of money. Jackass Banker combines real-world "know-how" with brilliant forecasting, as evidenced by Mr. Kelly's track record (http://jackassbanker.com/mr-kellys-publishedpredictions/).

Mr. Kelly appears at speaking events, offers portfolio management training classes and is actively involved with the financial markets.

Vol. II
A Colt Jackson Thriller & Adventure Story

Black Storm: Curse on the Caliphate

By: Robert L. Kelly

Robert L. Kelly's Black Storm: Curse on the Caliphate, Pits U.S. Navy SEAL Commander Colt Jackson Against an Islamic State Armed with Nuclear Weapons!

A sweeping story, Black Storm: Curse on the Caliphate takes place in the United States, the Caribbean, South America, Europe and, of course, the Middle East. Commander Colt Jackson, introduced in Mr. Kelly's last novel, Blood Moon Over D'Apocalypse™ is a Navy Seal who is asked to take on extraordinary missions.

In this second novel of the "Colt Jackson Thriller & Adventure Stories," Commander Jackson leads his SEALs against enemies who bring danger to the U.S. homeland. In this epic saga, the clever and diabolical leaders of the Islamic State (i.e. "ISIL") have engaged in a global scheme with one objective: the complete destruction of America. Their PhD leader and self-proclaimed Caliphate, Abu Bakr al-Baghdadi, a Sunni Muslim, has used his Mensa IQ to create an allegiance of axis powers. These include North Korea, Pakistan, Turkey, Qatar, Venezuela, as well as elements of the military and political powers, from China and Russia.

Abu Bakr, an avid student of Islamic history, will not strike America until ISIL is ready. When he does make a move, his genius mind has planned a death blow for the "Great Satan," using nuclear weapons---paving his way to a complete takeover of the Middle East.

In a non-stop action thriller, U.S. Navy SEALs, the NSA and the CIA must use every collective resource at their disposal to combat the brutal killers and murderers of ISIL. The intense drama and vivid writing of Mr. Kelly, makes for an exhilarating story. From hand-to-hand combat, advanced intelligence systems and weapons right out of Star Wars, the detailed research is artfully, and seamlessly, woven into the plot line.

Readers are taken into the inner circle of the NSA with a remarkable woman by the name of Lori Sanders, a brilliant and vivacious superstar---who happens to love Colt Jackson. Her quick mind and persistent commitment of service to country, is a female, mirror-image of Commander Jackson. Naturally, the sparks will fly!

"Black Storm" is a remarkable suspense novel, loaded with action, and is frighteningly realistic. Will Commander Colt Jackson save the day? Who will live and who will die? Only an unforgettable read will reveal the truth!

About The Federal Reserve Trilogy:

Mr. Kelly's warnings relating to the approaching credit crisis in 2007 and 2008 helped some people avoid devastating losses in their portfolios, because they took action *before* the crisis erupted. As everyone knows, ultimately, there was a complete stock-market meltdown and difficulty! In a "Déjà vu, all-over again" moment, Mr. Kelly is sounding the alarm bells EVEN LOUDER, yet another time.

The Federal Reserve Trilogy issues an urgent warning to all people and documents the causes, the motivations and the outcome of a devastating economic firestorm, called "D'Apocalypse™." It is swiftly approaching and set to strike nations all over the world. The trilogy unveils the secret plans of the bankers and global elite to collapse the financial system and seize control of the world's monetary policy and money supply systems. Mr. Kelly sleuths out the facts, figures, history, charts and patterns, revealing their master strategy, while compellingly providing nations, corporations and all wealth classes, specific recommendations to avoid disaster during this upcoming grab for power. The end result of D'Apocalypse™ will be social devastation and a severe economic meltdown, purposely caused by the bankers and the elite. It will rain ruin on hundreds of millions of people—with the onset of a dangerous and real global war, the likely result!

There are very few people, or organizations, with the ability to analyze and distill sets of complex information into understandable, tactical and easy-to-implement action plans. Mr. Kelly amply demonstrates these abilities, with the writing of The Federal Reserve Trilogy.

The $30 Trillion Heist—Scene Of The Crime?, and The $30 Trillion Heist—Follow The Money!, spell out how the banks, the Federal Reserve and the elite heisted nearly $30 Trillion from U.S. taxpayers—without the knowledge, or consent of Congress. Importantly, the books uncover what they are doing with this heist money. D'Apocalypse™ Now! unveils the logical conclusion and aftermath of the great heist. Reading it will help families, hedge funds, companies, and nations, avoid the worst of this purposely engineered, financial catastrophe.

Fortunes will be made and lost during the Great D'Apocalypse™ and The Federal Reserve Trilogy empowers you to assess the facts and compelling evidence, allowing you to make powerful and intelligent decisions during the course of the next several years. It is a set of books you will want to have in digital format because of their robust links, marvelous images, graphics and artwork. You may also want a hard copy for backup, just in case the lights go out and things really get bad!

A **Jack Assbanker**™ Publication

TABLE OF CONTENTS

INTRODUCTION

Robert Kelly's Federal Reserve Trilogy, written in 2013 and published in February 2014, comprised a breakthrough of investigative journalism on the subject of The Federal Reserve System, the great credit crisis, and the uncanny accuracy of Mr. Kelly's predictions for the financial markets.

The trilogy's first two books, The $30 Trillion Heist---Scene Of The Crime? and The $30 Trillion Heist---Follow The Money! describe in detail how the Federal Reserve, without authorization by Congress, provided the banks with a $30 Trillion secret bailout during the credit crisis. The third book, D'Apocalypse™ Now!---The Doomsday Cycle, forecasts our economic future as a result of this heist. Market forecasts were provided for the equity, precious metals, debt, and currency markets.

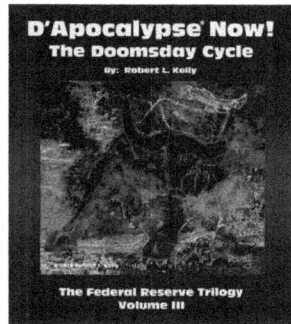

D'Apocalypse Now! accurately predicted the Dow would dramatically rise to between 22,000 and 37,000, when this index was trading in the 15,000's and most pundits were bearish. The Dow has since reached an interim high of 27,398.68 on July 13, 2019. The book also predicted a collapsing euro and a drop in the price of gold. The euro was trading at $1.3733/US Dollar and hit a temporary low of $1.0459 in early 2017, while gold was trading at close to $1,500/ounce and dropped to an interim low of $1,069.20/ounce on November 26, 2015.

The odds of being correct in the forecasts can be left to the odds-makers, but to say the odds were long would be an understatement.

Robert Kelly One of The Few
to Predict Dow 27,000---IN 2013!!!

New York, New York, September 23, 2015 (Newswire press release slightly edited for this book) D'Apocalypse Now! ---The Doomsday Cycle, was published February 19, 2014 by Jackass Banker (distributed at http://www.jackassbanker.com), Amazon, and Lightning Press (Ingram).

Predictions Fulfilled:

EURO: "Europe will be a major factor here. The euro will go bust." (par. 2 page 196). **Fulfillment:** The euro dropped from $1.3733 to $1.0459--- an ENORMOUS move in the currency markets.

GOLD: "...gold will drop below the first level of support at $1,196.67/oz. and the author believes as rates ratchet up and the dollar rallies, gold will drop even more." (par. 1 page 290). **Fulfillment:** Written in 2013, when nearly everyone was calling for gold to hit $5,000/ounce with trading in the $1,500 range, gold was $1,441.10 on publication date. The bottom dropped out and it hit a low of $1069.20 on November 26, 2015 for another big move in the futures markets. This move also triggered Mr. Kelly's Gold Purchase Price Target of $1,156.86. As of September 28, 2019, gold was $1,503.45/ounce. He saved investors 25.8% on the way down and made them 30% on the way back up.

CHINA: "China at risk of a bubble implosion, because of debt..." (par. 1 page 288). **Fulfillment:** A huge China scare in 2015 due to bad debt, as markets got rocked. China "reflated" the economy and the fat lady hasn't sung quite yet on the implosion, but cracks are showing.

DOW JONES: "Exit all positions by the end of May 2015." You should be OUT of all markets by the end of May 2015." (par. 4 page 314). **Fulfillment:** May 2015 was the absolute HIGH before a large, rapid correction hit the markets in August of 2015. This is when the Fed got scared and re-inflated the markets, once again. Page 304 clearly states in bold print "Buy The Dow" and on page 46, the book published a "Target Range" of 22,000-37,000 for the big push up.

##

Demacrash!

As a result of these unassailable, bold predictions <u>D'Apocalypse Now!</u> takes its place among the world's most insightful works on financial markets during the last five years. It virtually clobbers any pundit on television or in the media for accuracy.

<u>Demacrash!</u> provides investors and the general public critical information for the immediate future. Mr. Kelly lays out the coming knock-down, drag-out fight between Democrats and Republicans and its impact on financial markets.

The author's advice before reading this book is: "BUCKLE UP!"

His newly formulated detailed forecasts promise a page-turning race to act upon what is written, as peoples' fortunes are at stake. One thing is certain: the next decade will be one of the most volatile rides in financial history. If investments are not structured properly, people are destined to lose money, and a lot of it at that.

Mr. Kelly, as usual, puts it all on the line and provides detailed timelines of the financial future, as well as when to buy (and sell!) a variety of securities in a number of market sectors.

Beware, readers…

Politics is about to invade Wall Street like never before and <u>Demacrash!</u> is must reading to survive the 2020s!!

Praise for the Federal Reserve Trilogy

"*This explosive series of books is a must read for anybody who wants an insight into how our economy, our government and our very society is rigged in favor of the elite and against the average citizen, and has been for decades.*

With thorough research and documentation, Mr. Kelly removes the veil of mystery surrounding how the one percent has been exploiting the system at the expense of the average American---but, they don't stop there! D'Apocalypse Now!---The Doomsday Cycle, the third book in the Federal Reserve Trilogy, arms you with the signals to watch for and the strategies to implement yourself to turn things around. As the system continues to be dishonestly manipulated by insiders, you will not only be protected, but on the winning side!

With many of his forecasts already coming true, you can't afford to miss what Mr. Kelly has to say."

----Dave C.

"*WOW, what a great read! Outstanding information that allows the reader to peek into the Federal Reserve Banking System. Something this good, this thorough, cannot be missed. Kelly takes you through the creation and history of the Federal Reserve Bank and the Federal Reserve Act of 1913 that is easy to read and understand. I found the detail of Kelly's writing so unique and important that I utilized his full legal description of the Federal Reserve Act of 1913 in my own legal case that my own attorneys were unable to find. This book will literally set you free! Mr. Kelly, thank you and God Bless!*"

---Gary S.

CHAPTER 1

THE DEMOCRAT PLAN TO TAKE DOWN TRUMP

In the thick of political battle, in the thick of the fog of war, a plan emerges to defeat the enemy. As the world knows, the Democrats hate Donald Trump…he is the enemy…and they have a plan for war.

It is a Democrat's job, just like a Republican's, to get re-elected. This is part of politics. However, there are times in a nation's history when the vitriol and mud-slinging become so grave and the stakes become so high, a political party will do anything to get re-elected.

"Damn the torpedoes and full-speed ahead!" was first purportedly cried out in the heat of battle by Admiral David Glasgow Farragut who lived from 1801-1870. He commanded the vessel Hartford and witnessed numerous U.S. ships being sunk by Confederate "torpedoes" during the battle for Mobile in the Civil War. The torpedoes were actually tethered mines. (Source: https://www.wired.com/2009/06/mine-vs-cannon-vs-torpedo-in-high-speed-underwater-arms-race/).

With what appear to be numerous torpedoes in the water in the form of potential indictments (for political sabotage carried out during the 2016 election), the battle cry of Admiral Farragut might make a great Democrat campaign slogan for the next few years. They really have nothing to lose.

Demacrash!

The world has seen them fraudulently try to derail a man for the Supreme Court, try to take down the President himself, and they have stalled or blocked, every Trump Administration appointment possible. They are blind to the fact the public sees their skullduggery in an unfavorable light. With each and every failure, the Democrats continue to destroy their credibility. This is why they will lose badly in 2020.

The world knows they are using distraction, smoke-screen cover ups and illegal tactics. Many Democrat Party members potentially even committed grievous crimes in an attempt to win the high-stakes office of the Presidency and stay in power.

This book doesn't need to review all the things which smell like rotten fish, but some bear repeating: 1) evidence destruction of 30,000 emails; 2) people critical to key investigations winding up dead; 3) the leaking of classified information; 4) ballot "harvesting" and ballot-box stuffing; 5) the granting of immunities from prosecution by existing Democrats in power; 6) political appointees in sensitive positions using their power to destroy opposing political parties; and 7) the horrid double-standard being used to deal with what many consider to be crimes of high treason against the country (i.e. the spying on Donald J. Trump and his campaign, along with the political espionage happening before and after his election).

Many of these purported offenses are now under active investigation. If the Justice Department prosecutes anyone from the Democrat Party, a fireworks show extraordinaire will ensue. In fact, this show may be larger than the explosion once planned long ago by Guy Fawkes in the U.K. That man tried to blow up Parliament! Of course, successful prosecution presumes the Justice Department is unbiased, which most Americans know it is not. It is ensconced in its ranks with partisan Democrats.

Demacrash!

But make no mistake about it. If prosecutions are revealed, a beautiful Fourth of July celebration for Republicans shall unfold. However, there is a tremendous downside to this: it will cause the Democrats to become even more desperate for victory in the 2020 elections and beyond.

You see, Democrats *know* if they *don't* regain the White House and take the Senate many of their Party's leaders may be facing formidable actions by the U.S. Government, for years to come.

The stakes in 2020 and 2024 couldn't be higher, so…

"Damn the torpedoes, and full-speed ahead!"

Power for power's sake is natural in political war, but when one party has acted treacherously and treasonously against another (i.e. the act of trying to overthrow a duly elected President through political espionage)---and then gets caught---all hell should be expected to break loose.

It is also what is going to cause damage in a financial market near you. Why is this book certain of this? It's easy to understand.

Just ask *"What have the Democrat's achieved the last three years?"* Many readers may bluster and laugh, do some name calling, and perhaps even label the Democrats a do-nothing, resist-everything Party---except when it comes to spending money, increasing taxes and taking guns away.

But if you, as a reader, stated this opinion, you would be dead wrong. The Democrat's actually accomplished a great deal in the last several years:

**They took control of
the House of Representatives.**

Demacrash!

DEMOCRATS LEARNED FROM 2018'S MARKET CRASH

The question is, how exactly, did they accomplish this House victory?

Sure, there were issues of ballot stuffing and ballot harvesting in California and voted 8 Republicans out of office in the process. There was the live video feed from Miami capturing the hiding of ballot boxes (and the bringing in of *new* ballot boxes into the voting precincts in Dade County, Florida), among many other voting irregularities across the country. If you pointed to these practices and said, "*They likely had a material impact on elections,*" you wouldn't be wrong; but, the hard truth is while mid-term elections were happening, the stock market got crushed in 2018.

Just a coincidence? Perhaps---however, Demacrash! relies on its research and knowledge base to make market and political calls. These are the same disciplines which went into the writing of The Federal Reserve Trilogy.

More importantly, and looking forward, investors will likely experience a *massive* stock market rally,---with a serious correction along the way---before the major economic collapse and crash occurs. When will this crash happen? When will the correction occur?

The crash will likely occur in 2024, in the months before that year's Presidential elections. The fall of 2019 into 2020 looks ripe for a sharp correction (See Chapter 4 for detailed Market Forecast).

D'Apocalypse Now! stated the bankers would win the first tug of war in the markets after robbing the public of $30 Trillion and taking over trillions more in derivatives assets during the credit crisis. This has obviously come to pass as the markets have experienced massive asset inflation, as a result.

Demacrash!

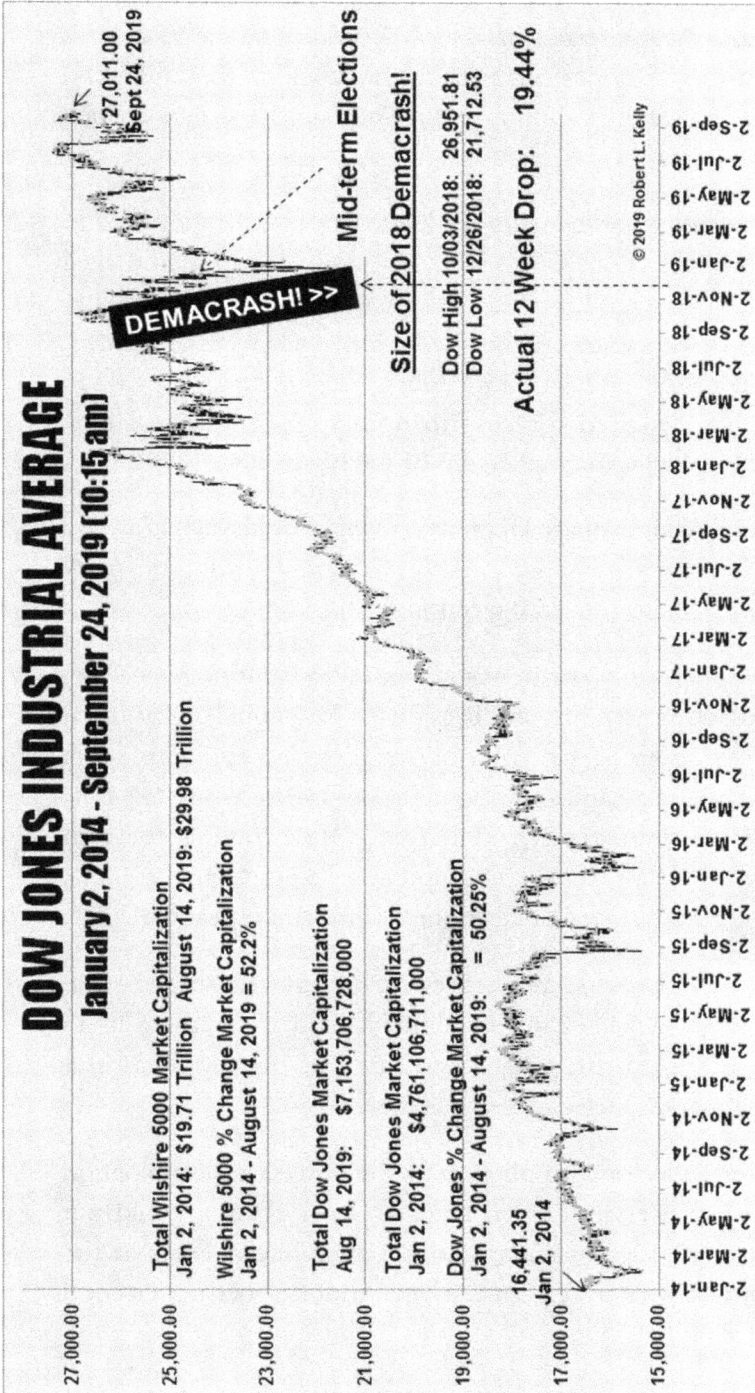

DOW JONES INDUSTRIAL AVERAGE
January 2, 2014 - September 24, 2019 (10:15 am)

27,011.00
Sept 24, 2019

Mid-term Elections

DEMACRASH! >>

Size of 2018 Demacrash!

Dow High 10/03/2018: 26,951.81
Dow Low: 12/26/2018: 21,712.53

Actual 12 Week Drop: 19.44%

© 2019 Robert L. Kelly

Total Wilshire 5000 Market Capitalization
Jan 2, 2014: $19.71 Trillion August 14, 2019: $29.98 Trillion

Wilshire 5000 % Change Market Capitalization
Jan 2, 2014 - August 14, 2019 = 52.2%

Total Dow Jones Market Capitalization
Aug 14, 2019: $7,153,706,728,000

Total Dow Jones Market Capitalization
Jan 2, 2014: $4,761,106,711,000

Dow Jones % Change Market Capitalization
Jan 2, 2014 - August 14, 2019:   = 50.25%

16,441.35
Jan 2, 2014

27,000.00
25,000.00
23,000.00
21,000.00
19,000.00
17,000.00
15,000.00

2-Jan-14
2-Mar-14
2-May-14
2-Jul-14
2-Sep-14
2-Nov-14
2-Jan-15
2-Mar-15
2-May-15
2-Jul-15
2-Sep-15
2-Nov-15
2-Jan-16
2-Mar-16
2-May-16
2-Jul-16
2-Sep-16
2-Nov-16
2-Jan-17
2-Mar-17
2-May-17
2-Jul-17
2-Sep-17
2-Nov-17
2-Jan-18
2-Mar-18
2-May-18
2-Jul-18
2-Sep-18
2-Nov-18
2-Jan-19
2-Mar-19
2-May-19
2-Jul-19
2-Sep-19

Size of 2018 Market Drop

As a result, the preferred assets of the rich and famous have been bid up, with enormous rises in the stock market, high-end real estate, collectibles, bonds, etc. The banks are now loaded with cash.

History teaches when bankers are loaded with cash, they love to stop lending and squeeze the markets---then swoop in and steal great assets for cheap prices. As many readers recall, this is exactly what happened in the credit crisis when Bear Stearns, Lehman Brothers and an entire mortgage industry were wiped out and then acquired for next to nothing. They are all now neatly tucked under the ownership of the big banks.

If one thinks like a smart Democrat, what would you do if you knew indictments were very likely coming against key party figures just prior to the 2020 elections?

The author knows what he would do, aside from making more outrageous claims against the President. He would *sprint* to JP Morgan, Goldman Sachs, Bank of America and Citibank, cut a deal and have the banks stop lending before elections (or slow lending down dramatically). Then have them dump stocks in the cyclically weak period in September and October 2020, leading into the November elections. Rinse and repeat for 2024.

These months provide perfect cover to unload securities in markets which quickly can turn illiquid---and when there is no liquidity, prices can drop hard and fast (on the flip side, in a raging bull market they can also rise incredibly).

This strategic decision to align with the banks, in combination with a Federal Reserve which hates Donald Trump, could put the squeeze on the President and the Republican Party at the right moment---beginning just a few months before election time.

Demacrash!

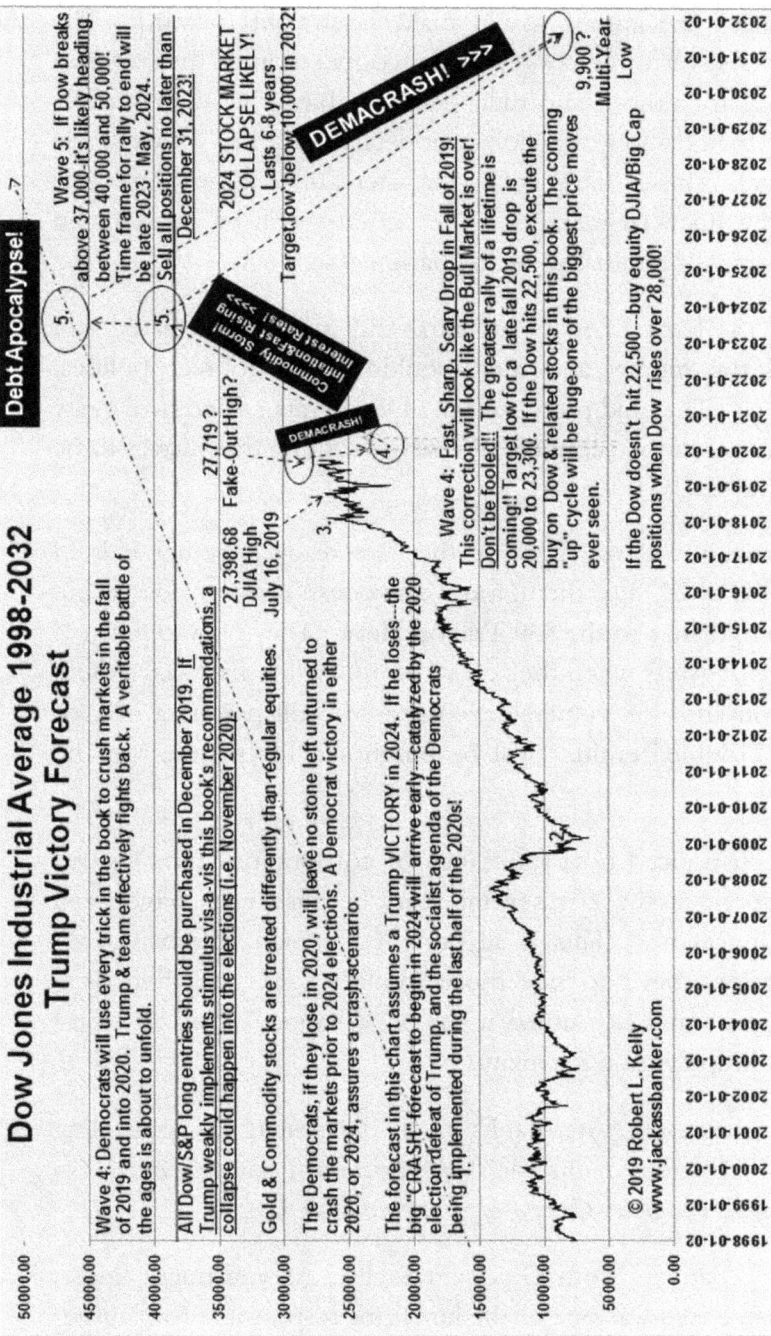

Dow Jones Industrial Average 1998-2032
Trump Victory Forecast

Debt Apocalypse!

Wave 4: Democrats will use every trick in the book to crush markets in the fall of 2019 and into 2020. Trump & team effectively fights back. A veritable battle of the ages is about to unfold.

All Dow/S&P long entries should be purchased in December 2019. If Trump weakly implements stimulus vis-a-vis this book's recommendations, a collapse could happen into the elections (i.e. November 2020).

Gold & Commodity stocks are treated differently than regular equities.

The Democrats, if they lose in 2020, will leave no stone left unturned to crash the markets prior to 2024 elections. A Democrat victory in either 2020, or 2024, assures a crash scenario.

The forecast in this chart assumes a Trump VICTORY in 2024. If he loses...the big "CRASH" forecast to begin in 2024 will arrive early---catalyzed by the 2020 election defeat of Trump, and the socialist agenda of the Democrats being implemented during the last half of the 2020s!

© 2019 Robert L. Kelly
www.jackassbanker.com

Wave 5: If Dow breaks above 37,000 it's likely heading between 40,000 and 50,000! Time frame for rally to end will be late 2023 - May, 2024.

Sell all positions no later than December 31, 2023!

2024 STOCK MARKET COLLAPSE LIKELY! Lasts 6-8 years

Target low below 10,000 in 2032!

DEMACRASH! >>>

27,398.68 DJIA High July 16, 2019

27,719 ? Fake-Out High?

Commodity Storm! Inflation Fast Rising Interest Rates! <<<

DEMACRASH!

Wave 4: Fast, Sharp, Scary Drop in Fall of 2019! This correction will look like the Bull Market is over! Don't be fooled!! The greatest rally of a lifetime is coming!! Target low for a late fall 2019 drop is 20,000 to 23,300. If the Dow hits 22,500, execute the buy on Dow & related stocks in this book. The coming "up" cycle will be huge-one of the biggest price moves ever seen.

If the Dow doesn't hit 22,500...buy equity DJIA/Big Cap positions when Dow rises over 28,000!

9,900 ? Multi-Year Low

7

Demacrash!

The "deal" the author would make is straight forward. The Democrats solicit the conspiratorial cooperation of the banks in exchange for power, and then grant the banks what they really desire: the creation of a global monetary authority with a single currency. This is likely to arrive after 2024, when panic sets upon the financial markets. The currency will be coordinated and effectively controlled by the banks.

This is the banks' and Democrats' end game. The banks can control the money and they wouldn't have to fear political blowback. The quid pro quo is the Democrats can control every single dollar in the economy, allowing anything that moves to be taxed and tracked.

The bankers will win because they are ready, whether it is in 2020 or in 2024. For them, four years doesn't matter. Banks are cash-rich, thanks to the $30 Trillion Heist. They plan to pick off some great assets when they create stress for the financial system and thousands of vulnerable companies collapse in a pile of debt. Troubled entities will be purchased for pennies on the dollar.

Have you noticed how thousands of corporations have loaded up on debt in the last several years because rates have been tantalizingly low? This is all part of the plan. Remember--- corporations have to pay those monies back. If there is a serious economic downturn, it will be "Chapter 7" and "Chapter 11" bankruptcy-time for many.

Is this realistic? Are banks really interested in controlling politics? A reader might ask, *"After President Trump won in 2016--- where did his initial key Cabinet appointments come from?"*

Answer: Bankers from Goldman Sachs. As you might know, Goldman Sachs was one of the key firms responsible for causing the credit crisis from 2007-2010. Its personnel have been tagged for key positions by each administration, ever since, in what appears to be cover-up control by the banks and their chief protector, the Federal Reserve.

President Trump's Chief Economic Adviser Gary Cohn (since departed from the Trump Administration) and Treasury Secretary Steve Mnuchin both hail from Goldman Sachs and were among the first people picked to lead the charge of the Trump Administration's finance team.

Timothy Geithner, former Chairman of the New York Federal Reserve (leading up to and during the credit crisis), became Treasury Secretary under the Obama Administration, while Hank Paulson, Treasury Secretary under Bush, was the former head of Goldman Sachs. In fact, on his watch as CEO of Goldman, mortgage-backed securities grew up, mushroomed and ultimately turned into a financial napalm bomb.

"Nail in the coffin" evidence which reveals the banks' illicit involvement with the Federal Reserve is reprinted in this chapter's section, "The $26 Trillion as Reported by the GAO".

The odds are quite fair Republicans (i.e. President Trump) also cut a deal of some kind with Wall Street based on who Trump hired as key financial advisers and winning the election against the odds. However, it looks like Democrats may have cut an even sweeter deal for the mid-term elections in 2018, given the stock market's timely fast-crash of nearly 20% before elections and the Democrat takeover of the House of Representatives.

While the ongoing skirmish between Fed Chairman Jerome Powell and President Trump is well documented, Fed alumni are also providing interesting insight into the Federal Reserve's true feelings toward President Donald Trump. This is major evidence of the Fed clearly throwing its support behind the Democrat Party. Somewhere, clearly, a deal has been cut.

Demacrash!

Bill Dudley, Vice-Chairman of the Federal Open Market Committee and former President of the New York Fed from 2009 to 2018, was also previously chief U.S. economist at Goldman Sachs. He recently proclaimed in a Bloomberg opinion-page article the Federal Reserve should *revolt* against President Trump.

> ### The Fed Shouldn't Enable Donald Trump
> The central bank should refuse to play along with an economic disaster in the making.
>
> U.S. President Donald Trump's trade war with China keeps undermining the confidence of businesses and consumers, worsening the economic outlook. This manufactured disaster-in-the-making presents the Federal Reserve with a dilemma: Should it mitigate the damage by providing offsetting stimulus, or refuse to play along?
>
> If the ultimate goal is a healthy economy, the Fed should seriously consider the latter approach. (Source: Bloomberg Opinion, https://www.bloomberg.com/opinion/articles/2019-08-27/the-fed-shouldn-t-enable-donald-trump, by Bill Dudley, August 27, 2019, 6:00 AM EDT)

Fed alumni don't say anything publicly that isn't being sung out of the same hymnal as their handlers. This article confirms a good probability the upcoming Presidential election for 2020 and 2024 will see some attempt to crash markets and put a Democrat in the White House---someone the Fed can control.

The Fed hates Donald Trump as much as the Democrats!

It is interesting to know who owns the New York Federal Reserve Bank. It is the key to running Federal Reserve Open Market Operations and can greatly influence financial markets. The following table shows since 1913, 44% of the New York

Demacrash!

Federal Reserve Bank has been gobbled up by JP Morgan Chase. This is due to a history of bank consolidations going back to the year the Fed was born in 1913.

The original shareholders in 1913 were derived from public data published by the New York Times at that time (as reprinted from The $30 Trillion Heist---Follow The Money!).

List of Member Banks Owning Stock In Federal Reserve Bank of New York

July 26, 1983 Owners Federal Reserve Bank of New York	Shares	Percent	As Of June 13, 2013 New Owners
National Bank of North America*	105,600	2%	Bank of America
Bank of New York	141,482	2%	Bank of New York Mellon
Citibank	1,090,813	15%	Citibank
European American Bank & Trust*	127,800	2%	Citibank
Subtotal Citibank		17%	
Bankers Trust Company	438,831	6%	JP Morgan Chase
Chase Manhattan Bank	1,011,862	14%	JP Morgan Chase
Chemical Bank	544,962	8%	JP Morgan Chase
Manufacturers Hanover	509,852	7%	JP Morgan Chase
Morgan Guaranty Trust	655,443	9%	JP Morgan Chase
Subtotal JP Morgan Chase		44%	
J. Henry Schroder Bank & Trust*	37,493	0.50%	No Change

Chart © 2014 Robert L. Kelly, based on Eustace Mullins original work, with updates by author.

Given the Fed's hatred for Trump and probable fact they are in bed with the Democrats---will the Democrats win in 2020?

Despite their intense distaste for the man, the author believes the Federal Reserve and Democrats will likely *fail* to dethrone the President in 2020.

In fact, Democrats may lose control of the House of Representatives, again. Reasonable people---even many of the bankers, see the far-left policies emanating across-the-board from existing Democrat candidates as highly dangerous, particularly to wealthy pocketbooks.

The bankers are smart enough to realize any deal they cut currently with a far-left leaning Democrat will likely be unwound once a Socialist Democrat comes to power.

From the bankers' perspective, it would be far better to have the Democrats on the ropes, desperate for a deal, and then strike a bargain which cannot be broken---even when leftists take power.

As discussed at length in <u>D'Apocalypse Now!</u> the bankers dream is to hijack the entire system by controlling a single currency, worldwide. Here is a brief excerpt from the book which may describe such events just over the horizon:

SATANIC BARGAIN-POLITICIANS, ELITE AND THE BANKERS

Naturally, there will be a quid pro quo---the politicians will be in a helpless state due to the utter impoverishment and distress among the people. The cacophony shall be so great from the populous the politicians will be SCREAMING, CRYING AND BEGGING the bankers and elite to turn on the supply of money and credit to get the markets moving again…

As part of this grand, satanic bargain, the banking elite will promise and guarantee to governments the capability to track and trace all transactions through the system, thereby allowing tax collections to be maximized. This will make the system become more severe, more efficient and create far greater revenues for the politicians, which will be music to the ears of spend-crazy politicos, worldwide.

With this coup-d'état of global monetary authority, the bankers will then have complete control over their ability to LEVERAGE the entire world's money supply into their monopoly-controlled, derivatives trading schemes—without government interference. This will provide the elite with a monopoly to control transactions, profits, and prices, worldwide across the derivatives and credit markets, as well as, over all real economies on earth.

Readers may be surprised the author is forecasting President Trump and the Republicans will win in 2020, given the "impeachment flavor du jour" at the moment, especially if the Democrats and the Fed are in bed with each other.

This is because of one huge error the Democrats made with the Trump Administration in 2019.

Nancy Pelosi and Chuck Schumer gave Trump the gift of providing an additional $324 Billion in discretionary spending, and the elimination of automatic spending cuts as part of the 2019 budget agreement. As approved by Congress and signed by the President, the spending bill removes the threat of default by the United States on its obligations until after the 2020 elections. As a result, financially speaking, President Trump has the wind at his back.

Because of this deal, Dems will likely lose in 2020, but will have gained more knowledge and experience in orchestrating economic problems for the 2024 elections.

Ultimately, the author expects a spectacular monetary and fiscal crash leading into and after, the elections in 2024. "You might regret what you wish for" may be words for Democrats to consider if they are planning to use scorched earth tactics. Democrats will have a financial catastrophe on their hands after the devil's deal with the banks and their victory in 2024.

But, for those seeking power, a crashing economy and a crashing market won't matter. The Dems will be completely desperate to take control and even if they knew in advance what their actions would bring, they would agree to anything with the banks and the Fed to decapitate Republicans "once and for all."

Because of this, Democrats would be fools to *not* try and cut a deal with the Federal Reserve and Wall Street for 2024. Whoever wins in 2024, will have cut a deal for sure.

This is precisely why the world will witness the emergence of a one-world currency from the rubble of the next crisis. It will be administered "jointly" with the banks (meaning, the banks will effectively be in control---just as the New York Fed is in charge of Open Market Operations at the Fed, which is effectively owned and controlled by JP Morgan Chase).

The Democrats may have cut a deal for 2020, no doubt. However, with no automatic spending cuts and an increase of a discretionary $324 Billion in the budget, Secretary Mnuchin and the President have plenty of ammunition to fight back. Market attacks can be defended with the President's Working Group on Capital Markets (i.e. "The Plunge Protection Team").

Given their ability to move money around and take advantage of the largesse of Nancy and Chuck, the Republicans have virtually unlimited firepower.

Along with breakthroughs in trade, the coming Trump policy decisions will contribute to the greatest bull market in history--- and witness its end. A last climatic climb to the top in the next several years will have everyone in the process thinking they were geniuses.

But, this will be the farthest thing from the truth.

The combined actions of decades of abysmal policy decisions by the Fed and politicians alike will lead to a tremendous bond crash, debt crisis and a stock market crash extraordinaire in the next major election cycle (i.e. 2024). The aftermath will be ugly.

By pouring cash into key financial markets over decades, with money printed out of thin air, the Federal Reserve caused financial asset inflation. The Federal Reserve Trilogy coined this "Assflation." This in turn, causes cost-push inflation in the supply chain because money in the hands of the elite gobbles up key assets. Prices rise due to asset acquisition costs and consolidation, while new pricing power is affected across global supply chains. It is good news for the super wealthy and very bad news for consumers. With fewer suppliers, pricing power and product availability is more tightly controlled by the wealthy.

Coming agricultural and product shortages in key staple supplies along with common stock shortages, are expected to create ever-increasing costs in supply chains around the world. Combined, these will likely cause the greatest increase in the inflation rate for basic necessities (i.e. rent, medical, food, clothing, etc.) in a century. Smaller packages and inferior materials disguise it.

Common stock inflation is a critical contributor to this growing problem because the wealth created by the stock market ultimately acquires tangible assets (e.g. real estate, hotels, food supply chains, commodities, etc.) at bid-up prices. Once acquired and consolidated with other assets---prices are driven up, in a quasi-monopolistic manner.

This is why "The rent is too damn high!" In major metropolises, a few large management companies have settled in and acquired or control rents of entire cities. The market has once again run faster than the government, and these miniature monopolies have caused vast increases in rent prices. All of these enterprises are controlled by the banks (i.e. nearly all the properties owned or managed carry large bank mortgages).

Working against inflation is the gigantic debt overhang of U.S. Dollars, worldwide. Overall, this debt is extremely deflationary and imported goods will drop in price---causing extreme pressure on domestic producers of competitive products.

Because of this complex economic tapestry being woven, one needs to be alert to radical change in certain sectors. This is how a reader will make money. This book should help you in identifying those changes and suggesting actions which may profit a reader handsomely, all the while pointing out a war of chaos between Republicans and Democrats.

In the discussion about shortages a few paragraphs ago, you might have wondered, *"How can there ever be a "shortage" of common stocks?"* In the case for a run to super-bull market highs, which this book predicts, the reason for the rally has its root cause in The $30 Trillion Heist; however, two additional new factors are impacting the marketplace:

1) The near-death experience, economically speaking of Europe, and most of the rest-of-the-world. This has bred a lack of confidence among big investors---even sovereign wealth funds. This is particularly true at major money-centers like Hong Kong, London, Singapore, Frankfurt, Paris, Tokyo and the entire Middle East. When the contagion hits, big money will move its capital *fast.* Capital will flow like water blasted through a fire hose to the U.S. debt and equity markets.

If there is war in the Middle East or even an invasion in parts of Asia---look for a panic in the Arab States. An invasion of Asia would also impact Singapore, and its "safe haven" status would be lost. If Pakistan and India go nuclear, or engage in a non-nuclear direct confrontation, expect monies (particularly from India) to flow to the U.S.

But, make no mistake: Europe is a sure thing. It is a basket case and is hiding behind negative interest rates. This horrid policy will turn and bite the E.U. directly on the behind.

Norway wealth fund should move more investment to North America, central bank says

 OSLO (Reuters) - Norway's $1 trillion sovereign wealth fund should shift billions in investments from European stock markets and instead invest more in the United States and other North American markets to seek higher returns, the fund's manager recommended on Tuesday. (Source: Reuters Business News, August 27, 2019, by Victoria Klesty and Terje Solsvik https://www.reuters.com/article/us-norway-swf/norway-wealth-fund-should-move-more-investment-to-north-america-central-bank-says-idUSKCN1VH0Z1).

The World's Most Fragile States

Results of the 2019 Fragile States Index (120 = highest fragility)

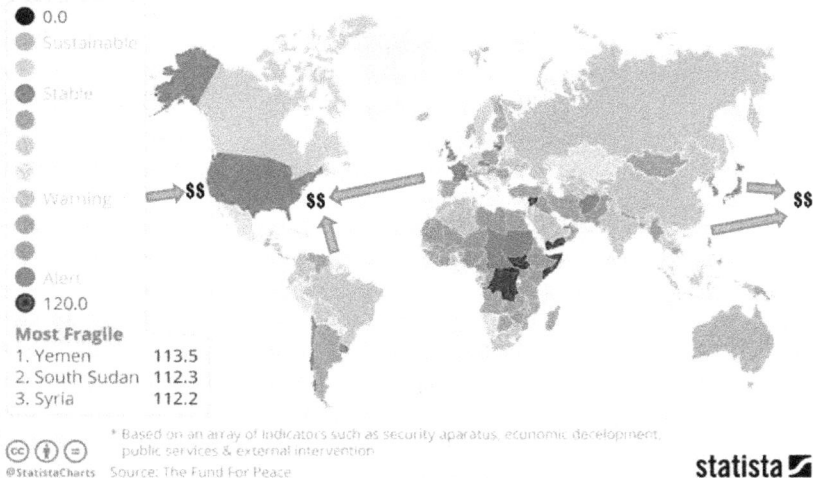

(Credit: "Mapping the World's Most Fragile States," by Tyler Durden, August 23, 2019, Zerohedge, Arrows & $$ signs by Robert Kelly).

2) Corporations primarily used the benefits of President Trump's and the Republican's tax-cut bill to repurchase common stock. These decisions create major liquidity issues for large sovereign wealth and hedge funds, when they decide "what" to buy in the stock markets in America as their markets head south. Bonds will not be a great option as interest rates will begin skyrocketing in 2020. Even if "official" rates on bonds are pegged at artificially low levels at the central banks, the corporate bond, junk bond, and emerging market sovereign bond rates will increase dramatically. Rising interest rates cause steep drops in the price of medium- and long-term bonds.

On the way up, a lack of liquidity is a great thing for equity investors in a bull market. Stock prices soar far beyond what anyone might think possible. In the coming great rally into 2024 big-cap stocks, because they offer the best option for liquidity, will be viewed as the last game in town for large, sophisticated investors. They require the ability to access their capital quickly, and will drive the stock market to the moon.

Ever since the Long Term Capital Management hedge fund disaster in 1998 nearly took down Wall Street and created the "Greenspan Put," politicians have needed to receive the ultimate blessing of Wall Street before they could get elected. Alan Greenspan has been perceived by many uninformed people as a "hero" for his actions during that crisis. Unfortunately, his easy-money policies merely kicked the problem down the road for someone else to clean up.

Since Mr. Greenspan, particularly, the tactic of using "easy money" has been the mantra of the Fed. This policy has been used during and after the credit crisis extensively. In 2007 when "Helicopter Ben" Bernanke, Chairman of the Federal Reserve, began his tenure and the credit crisis broke wide open, he architected a $30 Trillion Heist. He used U.S. Treasury securities and Fed credits backed by U.S. Taxpayers (without their permission and without the knowledge of Congress) to illegally bail out the banks with over $26 Trillion in unauthorized transactions.

This $26 Trillion secret bailout wasn't discovered until years after it took place, when the information was revealed in a General Account Office ("GAO) audit. See this chapter's pages 29-31.

Because of the history of the Federal Reserve's actions (i.e. giving trillions of dollars away exclusively to the rich, while letting the middle class and poor continue to be devastated with under-employment, inner-city devastation and rising costs on virtually all fronts), cities and states have been going bankrupt.

This is the real reason the media and many politicians want to race-bate. They failed in the false and fraudulent narrative of the Russian collusion hoax, and ongoing attempts to impeach the President by any means necessary, even if ridiculous.

These politicos and left-wing media types must point the finger *away* from themselves. Wealthy and well-paid reporters, along with their editorial staffs, are beholden to their "Mother-Ship" employers.

Since all of the media companies are owned, or controlled, by the banks---either through outright equity ownership, or via debt (as documented in The $30 Trillion Heist---Follow The Money!), employees have little choice. Read like a talking head---or find another job.

What better way to keep the public's nose out of a $30 Trillion Heist than to focus on nonsensical, untrue trains of thought and hyperbole---day, after day, after day. Unfortunately, this strategy of the elite is about to backfire, big time. 2025+ promises to see a revolt or even a civil war break out among the people---and the real reason: the money.

Rich people took it and poor people want it back. And make no mistake about it---both Democrats and Republicans were complicit in allowing the Federal Reserve to affect The $30 Trillion Heist (i.e. $26 Trillion + Quantitative Easing = Massive Assflation for the general population and wealth for the rich).

These facts may shed some light as to "why" we are hearing the spin we listen to everyday on television. Obviously, on a deeply personal level, Democrats hate Trump and want him out of office. But, the lengths to which they have gone defy anything in history and borders on the ludicrous.

The problem is, if the Democrats want to win they have to go back to the truth. Simply using communistic propaganda tactics will not work on the majority of Americans. Plenty of truth exists to destroy every sitting President since Ronald Reagan.

Right now, Democrats are the boy who cried wolf. Everyone snickers at their leadership's insane economic ideas, knowing this direction would turn America into Venezuela, overnight.

PRESIDENT REAGAN STARTED KICKING CAN DOWN ROAD
For the record, diehard Republicans and Reagan worshippers should know it was *President Reagan* who started kicking this financial bubble down the road when he "saved" the financial markets as they dropped 50% in the crash of October 19, 1987. The results of these actions became a "direct-dot" connection to Long Term Capital Management, Fed bailouts and the "Greenspan Put" just ten years later, as financial crisis erupted in August 1998.

You see, Ronald Reagan created the "Plunge Protection Team," formally named "The President's Working Group on Capital Markets." To this day, this group artificially supports and socializes losses in the stock and bond markets. This should never happen in a capitalist system, for the simple reason the main benefactor of this kind of support are rich people.

Ever since 1987 rents, tuition, medical expenses and the cost of basic necessities have skyrocketed for the average consumer, while real income has dropped for most people (particularly after 1998). There are now over 100 million people unemployed in the marketplace who are simply not counted by the U.S. Department of Labor.

Remember the previous generation of Americans? For most people, two parents didn't have to work to make ends meet. This is not the case anymore for 80% of the population which has suffered decades of abuse by the Fed. Today, both parents must work and society is suffering dramatically, as a result. Increases in violence, gang membership and corruption to its fullest, is the name of the game. When no one is home to watch the kids for decades, troubles show up on the door step.

FED'S ACTIONS HAVE DRIVEN UP COST OF LIVING
The bottom line is the Fed's actions have dramatically driven up the cost of living for everyone, but people living in the lower 80% of society have suffered the most; a lack of good jobs, lower relative incomes, and hardship have taken their toll on the masses---and the masses are beginning to take note.

To pour more salt on an open wound, the cost increases experienced by the 80% have not been captured in "trumped" up CPI data (i.e. Consumer Price Index). CPI data are in fact, a complete lie.

Twisting narratives by Administrations in power (e.g. Reagan, Bush, Clinton, Bush, Obama and now Trump) exist for the sole purpose it seems, of remaining in power. Along with the phony employment data published by the Department of Labor, people in the inner cities don't believe the inflation numbers touted by the government. In fact, most of them don't believe a word they hear from the Federal Government---and with good reason.

When you hear about unemployment figures at 3.6%---ask yourself why our government isn't counting over 100,000,000 people of working age who are able to work, in the calculation of the unemployed? This figure should be added to the numerator of that simple division problem. The results equal mass unemployment equal to those found in the Great Depression.

Instead, the Department of Labor discards these people and does not include them in the calculations. You can see why each and every President would have a tough time getting elected if the people knew real unemployment is hovering at the Great Depression rate of 34%.

THE FED PUSHED NEARLY EVERYONE INTO POOR HOUSE

Under the rule of the Federal Reserve, the rich haven't just gotten richer---they pushed everyone else into the poor house.

The elite are unaffected whether butter now costs $5 and rents have doubled. Rich people don't rent, they own, and their disposable income is enormous. Increased costs in electricity, food, rent, clothing, cars, education, etc. don't matter to them.

The problem is 80% of the population is hit hard by these cost-of-living increases. This is why Ben Bernanke and Janet Yellen are long gone from the halls of the Federal Reserve, garnering their huge consulting and speaking fees, and have passed the baton to Jerome Powell. They knew the jig was almost up and wanted to put some years between their departure from the Fed and the major blow ups coming to financial markets, worldwide. They are the direct result of their collective actions.

The Federal Reserve Board of Governors and the Federal Reserve Bank of New York Open Market Committee took the law into their own hands and bailed out the wealthy to the tune of $30 Trillion---when Congress had only authorized $700 Billion in TARP bailout money to battle the mortgage crisis.

This defines the heist of the century, and quite literally the greatest heist in the history of mankind.

The aforementioned situation is meticulously documented in The Federal Reserve Trilogy, Volume I, The $30 Trillion Heist, The Federal Reserve---Scene Of The Crime? Ironically, it is also the root cause of the real conundrum facing any President in power today, and the reason it is highlighted in this book.

The following passage is quoted from "Scene Of The Crime?" Current Fed Chairman Jerome Powell's smiling face can be seen as a member of the same Board of Governors as Ben Bernanke and Janet Yellen—the chief architects of the Heist.

U.S. and World Population Clock

Note: The Population Clock is consistent with 2010 Census data and the most recent national population estimates

May 02, 2013 12:53 UTC (-4)   Learn More 🔲 | Download and Share 🔲

🇺🇸 U.S. Population	🌍 World Population
3 1 5 , 7 8 2 , 0 8 ⁰	7 , 0 8 2 , 5 6 3 , 8 8 5

COMPONENTS OF POPULATION CHANGE		TOP 10 MOST POPULOUS COUNTRIES			
	12:53:01 UTC	1 China	1,349,585,838	6. Pakistan	193,238,868
One birth every 8 seconds		2 India	1,220,800,359	7. Nigeria	174,507,539
One death every 12 seconds		3 United tes	316,668,567	8. Bangladesh	163,654,860
One international migrant (net) every 44 seconds		4 Indonesia	251,160,124	9. Russia	142,500,482
Net gain of one person every 15 seconds		5 Brazil	201,009,622	10. Japan	127,253,075

(Source: U.S. Census Bureau, as retrieved from http://www.census.gov/popclock/)

Demacrash!

Secret Heist Decided by Only 7 Unelected People!

Without boring people who don't like looking at tables, please take a look at the Population Clock (Note: From 2010).

With over 300,000,000 people in the United States and over 7 billion people in the world, the omniscient (sarcasm intended) team of only 7 members on the Federal Reserve Board of Governors approved and delegated the authority to execute exchanges of worthless securities for U.S. taxpayer-backed monies through the Federal Open Market Committee ("FOMC") of the Federal Reserve Bank of New York, a private company. The FOMC also only consists of a very small number of unelected officials. They total only 12 people. However when one looks at many of the minutes published from FOMC meetings, only ten members appear present for voting---5 from the Federal Reserve Board of Governors and 5 members from the Reserve Banks, again, all of them underlined unelected officials.

It is this small group who took it in their own hands to *secretly* decide to *secretly* take nearly $30 Trillion of taxpayer-backed monies and give these monies away to the banks, the elite and even, potentially, to individuals. The recent amendments to the Federal Reserve Act, pushed through Congress by the Federal Reserve and its banking allies, reverses long-standing, protective covenants in the Federal Reserve Act to NOW allow payment and exchanges with INDIVIDUALS AND CORPORATIONS at the Federal Reserve banking window. This was *forbidden* in the original Act, as it tried to *prevent* this kind of potentially treacherous behavior from occurring.

The original writers of the Act knew if these actions were not prevented by law, there would be temptation to dip into taxpayer-backed monies to reimburse banks, businesses, as well as wealthy individuals, for poor business decisions. The Federal Reserve was NOT designed with this purpose in mind. Despite the law on the books at the time of the Credit Crisis, it appears the Fed window was used in a spectacularly egregious and nefarious manner (this book describes as The $30 Trillion Heist) to secretly reimburse banks, and elitists from devastating losses. This activity, of course, was also precisely ***against, and contrary to,*** the purpose and intent of the original writers of the Act.

To this day, there appear to be gross violations of multiple sections of the Federal Reserve Act by the Federal Reserve, the banks and the elite.

The bottom line is the members of the Reserve Board and 5 representatives from the Federal Reserve Banks decided surreptitiously to secretly give away nearly $30 Trillion to banks and rich people, without approval from Congress, when billions of people on the world population clock are starving and tens of millions of Americans are out of work!

This is a travesty and shocking crime against humanity and the country, in this writer's opinion.

Ben S. Bernanke
Chairman

Janet L. Yellen
Vice Chair

Elizabeth Duke

Daniel Tarullo

Demacrash!

| Sarah Bloom Raskin | Jeremy C. Stein | Jerome H. Powell |

Collectively, these are the people responsible for making the decision to give away nearly $30 Trillion to the banks and the elite:

Members of the Federal Reserve Board During The Great Heist

They, in turn, delegate the operational authority through the Federal Open Market Committee and the New York Federal Reserve Bank to conduct the open market operations to exchange the banks' bad paper for U.S. taxpayer-backed money. There are supposed to be twelve members on the FOMC, with the New York Federal Reserve Bank having a permanent seat on this Committee. 2013 Members of the FOMC are:

Federal Reserve Board Members	Federal Reserve Banks (4 Rotate)
Ben S. Bernanke, Board of Governors, Chrmn	William C. Dudley, New York, Vice Chrmn
Elizabeth A. Duke, Board of Governors	James Bullard, St. Louis
Jerome H. Powell, Board of Governors	Charles L. Evans, Chicago
Sarah Bloom Raskin, Board of Governors	Esther L. George, Kansas City
Jeremy C. Stein, Board of Governors	Eric S. Rosengren, Boston
Daniel K. Tarullo, Board of Governors	
Janet L. Yellen, Board of Governors	

(Source: The $30 Trillion Heist Scene Of The Crime?, Chapter 6, pages 97-99).

The following are the minutes from the FOMC meeting in 2007 authorizing the acceptance of home mortgages as collateral, which was not authorized in The Federal Reserve Act:

Demacrash!

Meeting Held By the Federal Open Market Committee on September 18, 2007:

A meeting of the **Federal Open Market Committee (emphasis added)** was held in the offices of the Board of Governors of the Federal Reserve System in Washington, D.C., on Tuesday, September 18, 2007 at 8:30 a.m.

Present:
Mr. Bernanke, Chairman
Mr. Geithner, Vice Chairman
Mr. Evans
Mr. Hoenig
Mr. Kohn
Mr. Kroszner
Mr. Mishkin
Mr. Poole
Mr. Rosengren
Mr. Warsh"
Author comment: others in attendance included a host of support staff and other officials from the Federal Reserve.

'...On August 17, the FOMC issued a statement noting that financial market conditions had deteriorated and that tighter credit conditions and increased uncertainty had the potential to restrain economic growth going forward. The FOMC judged that the downside risks to growth had increased appreciably, indicated that it was monitoring the situation, and stated that it was prepared to act as needed to mitigate the adverse effects on the economy arising from the disruptions in financial markets. Simultaneously, the Federal Reserve Board announced that, to promote the restoration of orderly conditions in financial markets, it had approved a 50 basis point reduction in the primary credit rate to $5\frac{3}{4}$ percent. The Board also announced a change to the Reserve Banks' usual practices to allow the provision of term financing for as long as thirty days, renewable by the borrower. *In addition, the Board noted that the Federal Reserve would continue to accept a broad range of collateral for discount window loans, including home mortgages and related assets, while maintaining existing collateral margins'* (Source: The $30 Trillion Heist---Follow The Money, page 235).

THE FED'S REVERSE ROBIN HOOD ECONOMICS

We know the aftermath of what occurred. The banks grew richer and 40 million people lost their homes (a black-letter fact). Living costs and inflation have skyrocketed---despite what the CPI indicates---while wages for 80% of the population have remained stagnant. But, the Fed and its bevy of commentators cheer: "Yes, but we saved the banks." This is really outrageous. The beauty of real capitalism and not socialized capitalism for the rich is bad companies are rooted out and new investors step in! The Fed just took care of the club. This system of Reverse Robin Hood Economics is what the Democrats, and anyone else, should be fighting against.

The violence we are witnessing across the nation is not only because of race and politics. As the reader may now understand, one of the main reasons why violence is rearing its ugly head today is because of money. It is as clear as day: Rich people, mostly white, were the benefactors of $30 Trillion stolen from the people and the people are pissed off and want it back, even if they don't know it yet.

The oppressed know something has changed and are acting out as a direct result.

The cries by millions of people for socialism should be a wake-up call to the greedy. The Federal Reserve also believes in socialism but, apparently only for rich people. They socialized 100% of the banking losses via the $30 Trillion Heist, and used socialism for the rich to layer hidden taxes on the people to pay for it. These changes are now being felt through increasing costs in the economy and a growing revolt brewing among the people.

In their gut, deep down, regular people know something isn't quite right. As politician Jimmy McMillan has screamed hundreds of times when he has run for elected office over the years, and as stated previously in this book:

"The rent is just too damn high!"

People know costs have risen dramatically and good jobs are scarce, hardly an America the majority of people grew up in.

If you want to learn more about the $30 Trillion illegally taken to secretly bail out the banks and the evidence and concrete proof the author uncovered to PROVE it, read The $30 Trillion Heist---The Federal Reserve---Scene of the Crime?

The evidence is beyond strong: the "smoking gun" was found buried deep within the bowels of an arcane hundred+ page report by the General Accounting Office ("GAO"). Copies of these and many other documents were published in the three books of The Federal Reserve Trilogy.

THE $26 TRILLION AS REPORTED BY THE GAO: THE FIRST $16 TRILLION TO THE BANKS

Note both national and *international* banks received TRILLIONS!

The tables, which follow, are in $ BILLIONS (e.g., Citigroup was given $2,513,000,000,000 ($2.513 Trillion!).

Table 8: Institutions with Largest Total Transaction Amounts (Not Term-Adjusted) across Broad-Based Emergency Programs (Borrowing Aggregated by Parent Company and Includes Sponsored ABCP Conduits), December 1, 2007 through July 21, 2010

(Source: "FEDERAL RESERVE SYSTEM Opportunities Exist to Strengthen Policies and Processes for Managing Emergency Assistance," GAO-11-696 Federal Reserve System, page 131).

Dollar in billions Borrowing Parent Company	TAF	PDCF	TSLF	CPFF	Subtotal	AMLF	TALF	Total loans
Citigroup Inc.	$110	$2,020	$348	$33	$2,511	$1	-	$ 2,513
Morgan Stanley	-	1,913	115	4	2,032	9	-	2,041
Merrill Lynch & Co.	0	1,775	166	8	1,949	-	-	1,949
Bank of America Corporation	280	947	101	15	1,342	2	-	1,344
Barclays PLC (United Kingdom)	232	410	187	39	868	-	-	868
Bear Stearns Companies, Inc.	-	851	2	-	853	-	-	853
Goldman Sachs Group Inc.	-	589	225	0	814	-	-	814
Royal Bank of Scotland Group PLC (United Kingdom)	212	-	291	39	541	-	-	541
Deutsche Bank AG (Germany)	77	1	277	-	354	-	-	354
UBS AG (Switzerland)	56	35	122	75	287	-	-	287
JP Morgan Chase & Co.	99	112	68	-	279	111	-	391
Credit Suisse Group AG (Switzerland)	0	2	261	-	262	0	-	262
Lehman Brothers Holdings Inc.	-	83	99	-	183	-	-	183
Bank of Scotland PLC (United Kingdom)	181	-	-	-	181	-	-	181
BNP Paribas SA (France)	64	66	41	3	175	-	-	175
Wells Fargo & Co.	159	-	-	-	159	-	-	159
Dexia SA (Belgium)	105	-	-	53	159	-	-	159
Wachovia Corporation	142	-	-	-	142	-	-	142
Dresdner Bank AG (Germany)	123	0	-	10	135	-	-	135
Societe Generale SA (France)	124	-	-	-	124	-	-	124
All other borrowers	1,854	146	14	460	2,475	103	62	2,639
Total	$3,818	$8,951	$2,319	$738	$15,826	$217	$71	$16,115

Source: GAO analysis of Federal Reserve System data.

(Source: As retrieved from http://www.gao.gov/products/GAO-11-696, page 131).

"To place $16 trillion into perspective, remember that GDP of the United States is only $14.12 trillion. The entire national debt of the United States government spanning its 200+ year history is "only" $14.5 trillion. The budget that is being debated so heavily in Congress and the Senate is "only" $3.5 trillion. Take all of the outrage and debate over the $1.5 trillion deficit into consideration, and swallow this Red pill: There was no debate about whether $16,000,000,000,000 would be given to failing banks and failing corporations around the world.

In late 2008, the TARP Bailout bill was passed and loans of $800 billion were given to failing banks and companies. That was a blatant lie considering the fact that Goldman Sachs alone received 814 billion dollars. (author's emphasis) As, it turns out, the Federal Reserve donated $2.5 trillion to Citigroup, while Morgan Stanley received $2.04 trillion. The Royal Bank of Scotland and Deutsche Bank, a German bank, split about a trillion and numerous other banks received hefty chunks of the $16 trillion." (Source: "Audit of the Federal Reserve Reveals $16 Trillion in Secret Bailouts,"byIam1ru1-2, unelected.org, 12/27/2011, retrieved from http://www.freerepublic.com/focus/f-news/2825696/posts)

$10 TRILLION HANDED OUT TO FOREIGN BANKS

An additional $10 Trillion was handed out to foreign banks (Source: "FEDERAL RESERVE SYSTEM Opportunities Exist to Strengthen Policies and Processes for Managing Emergency Assistance" GAO-11-696, page 205, as retrieved from http://www.gao.gov/products/GAO-11-696):

Use of Dollar Swap Lines by Foreign Central Banks

Table 24 lists the foreign central banks in order of the aggregate amount of dollars drawn under the swap line arrangements with FRBNY. The European Central Bank received the largest amount of dollars under the swap line arrangements. Banco do Brasil, Bank of Canada, Monetary Authority of Singapore, and the Reserve Bank of New Zealand did not draw on their swap lines. The European Central Bank accounted for about 80 percent of total dollars drawn under the swap lines.

Table 24: Foreign Central Banks' Use of Dollar Swap Lines by Aggregate Dollar Transactions

Dollars in billions

Rank	Central bank	Number of transactions	Aggregate dollar transactions	Percent of total
1	European Central Bank	271	$8,011	79.7%
2	Bank of England	114	919	9.1
3	Swiss National Bank	81	466	4.6
4	Bank of Japan	35	387	3.9
5	Danmarks Nationalbank (Denmark)	19	73	0.7
6	Sveriges Riksbank (Sweden)	18	67	0.7
7	Reserve Bank of Australia	10	53	0.5
8	Bank of Korea (South Korea)	10	41	0.4
9	Norges Bank (Norway)	8	30	0.3
10	Banco de Mexico	3	10	0.1
	Total	**569**	**$10,057**	**100.0%**

Source: GAO analysis of Federal Reserve Board data.

Note: Foreign central banks not included in this table did not draw dollars under their swap line agreement with FRBNY. Aggregate dollar transactions represent the sum of all dollars drawn under the swap line arrangements and have not been adjusted to reflect differences in the terms over which the dollar draws were outstanding.

Unfortunately, this outright theft of money was promptly swept under the carpet by the then-sitting Congress, U.S. Senate and U.S. Justice Department, despite potentially serious violations of law and, as seriously questioned by the GAO in its report.

Given this extensive background, readers can understand Wall Street has "ginormous" sums of money and is willing to spend hundreds of millions of dollars (maybe even a Trillion!) to make sure they are not impacted too much, by political events. The Democrats they know will come running to them.

THE DEMOCRATS DEAL WITH THE BANKS

The trail of bread crumbs leads one to believe Democrats must have cut a deal with the Fed and the major banks for the mid-term elections in 2018. The fast-crash in the fall of 2018, when the stock market dropped 18.7% from October 3, 2018 to December 24, 2018, seemed like a too-convenient shellacking just before and after elections on November 6.

Whether the Democrats learned by watching this situation unfold before their eyes and regained the House by "coincidence," or were actively involved in this mini-crash, makes no matter. The Democrats will stop at nothing to gain power and they learned a real-life lesson from the fall of 2018:

Democrats now believe they can gain seats in Congress when markets CRASH in scary fashion at election time.

In 2020, however, they will likely fail to take control. In fact, a major rally is expected to start in 2020 which will ultimately complete the original forecast in <u>D'Apocalypse Now!</u> It will end likely sometime in 2024 (i.e. "Sell in May and go away…"), with the Dow expected to rise up to 37,000, or higher.

What better way to *try* and beat Donald J. Trump than to destroy his sacred stock market rally, just before elections, through a deal with the Fed and the banks. The Democrats will certainly try and crush the markets in 2020, you can bet on it, but given

Nancy and Chuck's budget mistake, they will fail.

But Democrats, be of good cheer---the collapse and chaos expected from 2024-2030 (at least) will be nothing but treacherous and a nightmare for Republicans entering the 2024 elections.

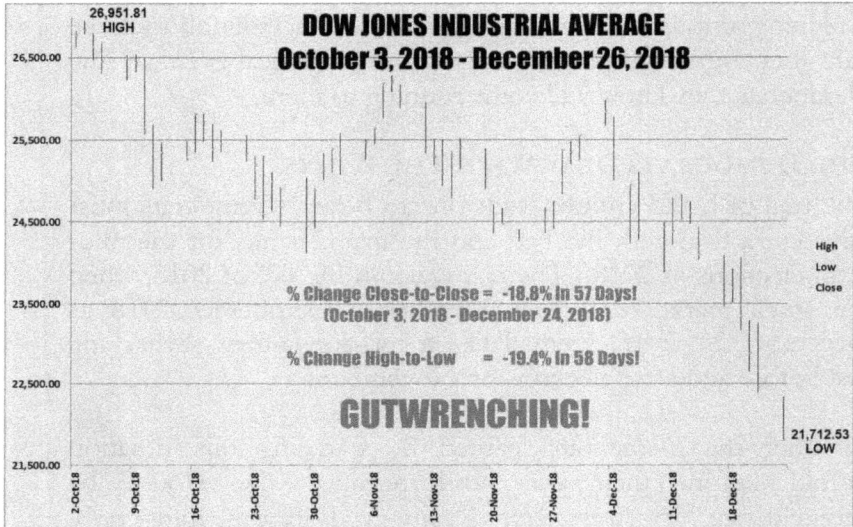

DOW JONES INDUSTRIAL AVERAGE
October 3, 2018 - December 26, 2018

26,951.81 HIGH

% Change Close-to-Close = -18.8% In 57 Days!
(October 3, 2018 - December 24, 2018)

% Change High-to-Low = -19.4% In 58 Days!

GUTWRENCHING!

21,712.53 LOW

Don't listen to the talking heads on TV, watch the market, it will tell you who is winning.

The author's betting on Trump to win in 2020, but the Democrats will (and should if they want victory) call the bankers and sympathetic Fed members into a back room---and make them an offer they cannot refuse---likely for 2024.

The offer and acceptance will send the country into bedlam, but the Dems will gain their power. Only time will tell if the bold predictions in this book are true, but make sure you bring the popcorn, because events over the next several years will be nothing but interesting.

CHAPTER 2
ESREVER NIBOR DOOH SCIMONOCE

Translation: Reverse Robin Hood Economics. The Trump Administration has the ability to fight back hard against this predicted Democrat onslaught.

The Democrats, as discussed in Chapter 1, made an enormous strategic blunder when Nancy Pelosi and Chuck Schumer agreed to a budget with the Trump Administration and eliminated all automatic budget cuts which were previously a matter of law. They also provided the Trump Administration with a $324 Billion increase in discretionary spending, providing it with $1.37 Trillion in fiscal year 2020. That is a whole lot of financial firepower.

With the ability to move money around within the budget, along with control of The President's Working Group on Capital Markets, the Trump Administration can fight back at will against Democrat attacks during the 2020 elections.

This will not be the case for 2024 however, because the 2019 budget deal was only for two years through the 2020 election .

Also for 2020, the Fed is in a quandary. Given the continuing drumbeat of President Trump and his war dance against the Federal Reserve (i.e. they rose interest rates too fast, they are using too much quantitative tightening, etc.), the Fed is in the uncomfortable position of having a very unfavorable light shed on it.

Given their hatred for Trump, there is probably nothing better they would like to do than completely kill the markets and tighten monetary policy. Unfortunately, this would mean Jerome Powell would be left "holding the bag," assuring Bernanke and Yellen will make good on their escape from the great $30 Trillion Heist, with Powell to blame for any meltdown in the markets.

If Mr. Powell kills liquidity, this would be a career-ending move for him, unless he has a golden parachute of an escape plan. This is why his immediate response to the sky-high overnight REPO rate crisis the week of September 15, 2019 was to flood the market with liquidity. For those who don't know, the overnight "REPO" rate soared to 10% from about 2% in one night. It is the inter-bank lending rate. This unexpected and rapid, pulsating rise is a clear warning shot about what this book is predicting for interest rates in the future. They will rise dramatically because central banks, worldwide, artificially kept rates low, flooded rich people with money, while governments spent like there was no tomorrow. This will cause the greatest debt crisis in human history.

Powell is in a box, which is looking more like a coffin with each and every day. Very few people remember he wasn't alone in the creation of his morbid resting place.

Properly orchestrated and in a full-blown Fed squeeze, likely in 2024, the banks will be in position for the greatest benefit of all. By then, Powell will have finished his term, there will be no more budget deal, and the Fed will have the perfect patsy to blame for markets crashing---a Trump-appointed Chairperson not on the Federal Reserve Board of Governors during the credit crisis.

When the real tightening cycle begins, the banks on cue will call in loans and refuse to advance credit. No mortgage loans will be made available either, and prices will crash nearly across the board. Real estate will be hit very hard by these actions, as will many overleveraged, enormous companies. They are key asset targets of the banks in this crashing credit cycle---along with marquis investment properties in New York and other "tall" cities.

This sounds like a repeat of the credit crisis, but this time unlike then, the banks are ready. Ben Bernanke, Janet Yellen, Jerome Powell and Timothy Geithner and others serving on the FOMC committee in 2007 made sure of that.

Whether or not the ultimate swoop down and pillage of the economy occurs in 2020, or in 2024 beginning in the January-May timeframe, makes no real difference to the bankers.

The bankers' next targets are enormous corporations, newly completed billionaire towers and pristine assets of countries (e.g. ports of entry, national parks, toll infrastructures, geological drilling rights, etc.). The bankers will focus on centers of influence and power over the civilian population along with those products and services offered by over-leveraged companies which will benefit from oligopoly-like pricing power, once they are seized.

Which industries will be affected? This is a great question. One which comes to mind is the oil industry, where many companies carry a great deal of debt. When rates go up and they need to refinance (perhaps occurring as oil prices drop), the banks will be hanging a sign outside their door which reads: "No habla Ingles!"

A glance through this book's later chapters will point the way. In chapters 4-8 a large number of securities and currencies are listed which may be good investments. Easy-to-understand table formats were used to help investors during this turbulent period.

THE DEBT CONUNDRUM

As you might imagine, most really "smart" Chief Financial Officers have whispered into their CEO's ear, "*Hey boss…lets borrow some money…it only will cost us 2%, and then we can buy back our common stock in the open market. Our share price will go to the moon and our earnings-per-share numbers will be golden. We'll surely hit our bonus numbers, then!"*

Today, these people look like geniuses. Stock prices are up, debt payments are low and they can always refinance---or so they think.

Tomorrow, however, these same really "smart" CFOs and CEOs will be blamed for failures of gigantic proportions because many companies, including some in the Fortune 100, will find themselves burned to the ground by debt.

The monetary system is about to change radically with escalating interest rates and the inability to refinance loans. Collapse of lumbering corporate giants will come fast and hard, exactly like it happened to Lehman Brothers and Bear Stearns during the credit crisis.

The fast collapse will be "caused" by rising interest rates, a bullish U.S. dollar, the inability to refinance balance sheets and a cruel economic downturn.

Astronomically high interest rates will cripple what used to be fine companies. Overnight, literally, lines of credit will be shut down.

To prevent this catastrophe from happening to a company near you, any Fortune 1000 CFO (or any country, or local government) should be *selling* 30-, 50- and 100-year bonds and locking in the historically low rates found today in the marketplace.

If you observe the corporate bond market, rates are rising back up in the world. Recently, even Germany couldn't sell long-term bonds at low interest rates and had to abandon an auction. The jig is nearly up for the Europeans.

Demacrash!

Germany Regrets Size of Bond That Pays Nothing as Auction Flops

Debt agency admits sale of 2050 bond may have been 'too large.' Getting paid to borrow draws new attack from Trump on Fed. (Source: Bloomberg Business News, https://www.bloomberg.com/news/articles/2019-08-21/germany-sees-anemic-demand-for-30-year-bond-sale-at-zero-coupon, by John Ainger, August 21, 2019).

Corporations and countries with great debt should DEFINITELY refinance today at a 30-year rate, or longer, if possible. Corporate debt many times is shorter term. Huge companies making multi-billion dollar acquisitions, often take on tens of billions of dollars in near-term debt (i.e. 1-5 years) to get a deal done. For example, the Walt Disney acquisition of Fox, consummated March 20, 2019, left Disney with between $16-$17 Billion dollars in debt, while Bayer's taking over Monsanto on June 19, 2018 saw the issuance of €5 Billion euros in debt with a four-year maturity. There are hundreds of other examples of companies at risk. They will discover it will not be easy to refinance in the years ahead.

All companies should be restructuring and refinancing their debt with much longer terms. Yes, by doing so they would pay a little more interest; however in the process, they would save their corporation from the ravages of steeply rising interest rates, and the high probability of risk associated with refinancing in years ahead.

A CFO's and CEO's job is to look to the future, but many wind up managing for their yearly bonus numbers, which are often tied to stock price. By refinancing to long-term bonds immediately, these people would save their companies in the long term. Right now, the author predicts just as the monetary crisis and debt collapse goes into full swing, these debt-laden companies will be the new "prey" of the big banks and the elite. Thinking Board members should be making changes at the top now, if managing a debt-heavy company.

Demacrash!

D'Apocalypse Now! and The $30 Trillion Heist explain in detail how the big banks, in collusion with the Fed, caused a credit squeeze and panic at both Lehman Brothers and Bear Stearns. Each of these once fine Wall Street firms sold for next to nothing to the big banks. Among the major beneficiaries were JP Morgan Chase, Barclays and competitors of these two firms (e.g. Goldman Sachs, Morgan Stanley, Bank of America, Citigroup, etc.).

> JP Morgan Chase stole the company based on true value, as Bear Stearns was sitting on extremely valuable assets---it owned the Street's most prestigious clearing-firm business, it had over $300 Billion in assets on its balance sheet *and it had $13.7 Trillion in derivatives* transactions on its books! The lesson here is ANY company with tremendous assets can fail---especially if you cannot renew your credit lines. (Source: The $30 Trillion Heist---The Federal Reserve---Follow The Money! page 94 by Robert Kelly).

> JP Morgan Chase, one of the largest, original founders of the Federal Reserve System, acquired $66.7 Billion in assets + $13.7 Trillion in derivatives + $28 Billion in Level 3 assets + $30 Billion in cash from the U.S. taxpayer---all for the mere pittance of $1.2 Billion in stock, which would have been only $200 million in stock if the Bear Stearns shareholders hadn't screamed to high heavens! (Source: ibid, page 98).

When markets turn down and the debt tsunami arrives, once "smart" CFOs will reach out to their friendly banker seeking an extension on their company's loan, or line of credit. As with Lehman Brothers and Bear Stearns, the banks will decline. Then, they will circle their prey and go in for the kill, just like vultures.

Interest rates in the corporate debt and emerging-market sovereign bond markets should rise and accelerate after 2020 begins, if not sooner, and they will soar into the 2020's. Interest rates have built a launch pad ready for lift off, given the Fed's artificial interest-rate engineering. The REPO rate scare was merely a warning shot.

All the while when "real" market rates accelerate, the Fed's "official" bank rate, reserved for only the banks and preferred persons of the elite, could remain low---or even negative. Yes, unfortunately, Congress changed the law after the credit crisis to allow "individuals" approved by the Fed to borrow and operate at the Fed window---as documented in The Federal Reserve Trilogy. The Fed window was never originally intended to be open to wealthy individuals (or partnerships, or corporations):

-CITE-
12 USC Sec.343   1/15/2013

-EXPCITE-
TITLE 12-BANKS AND BANKING
CHAPTER 3-FEDERAL RESERVE SYSTEM
SUBCHAPTER IX – POWERS AND DUTIES OF
FEDERAL RESERVE BANKS

-HEAD-
Sec. 343. Discount of obligations arising out of actual commercial transactions

-STATUTE-
-MISC1-
                    AMENDMENTS
        2010 – Pub. L. 111-203, Sec. 1101(a)(1)-(4) designated second par. as par. (3)(A), substituted "any participant in any program or facility with broad-based eligibility" for "any individual, partnership, or corporation…"
(Source: U.S. Congress statute, as cited. Reprinted from The $30 Trillion Heist---The Federal Reserve---Follow The Money, by Robert L. Kelly, page 138 & 142).

The change in the law won't matter, however, unless you are a bank, or a preferred customer of the Fed. Regular corporations will pay market prices for *their* loans, causing many to go belly up.

This rate pressure will put corporations, the U.S. Government and Fed in a serious bind. Because of the artificial interest-rate engineering by the Fed and other central banks (i.e. keeping rates artificially low for decades), there will be few real buyers of major governmental financings in the 2020s.

The central banks will be left with the only alternative they have--- monetize the debt. The Fed in its case, through a network of phony Caribbean Island bank accounts along with Fed guarantees to smaller countries (e.g. Denmark), will purchase the U.S. Government's own debt at auction---and in the aftermarket.

This may fund the U.S. Treasury, but it will create tremendous monetary, cost-push inflation, which is already severe for the general population. Because of the Fed's long history of "socialism for the rich" bailout policies, and irresponsible government spending, a civil war will erupt in the 2020s.

A battle will emerge between the "haves" and the "have-nots," and not even CNN will be able to spin this confrontation into a racist moment, unless they spin it with the color green.

The alternative is if the Fed allows interest rates to rise with market conditions, then the U.S. Government will quickly go broke. The Fed's choice will be to either let rates at the Fed rise with the market, or monetize their debt needs and create massive inflationary pressure in the system.

Either way, the government is screwed!

As you can see, the "debt clock" went over $22 Trillion (as retrieved August 14, 2019 12:10 pm, https://www.usdebtclock.org/).

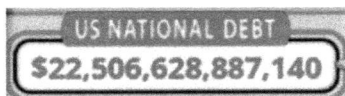

US NATIONAL DEBT
$22,506,628,887,140

Demacrash!

U.S. and World Population Clock

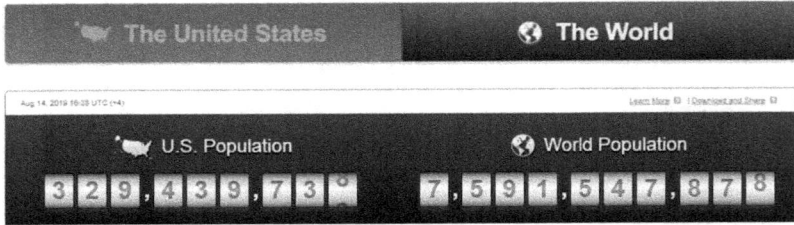

| The United States | The World |

| U.S. Population | World Population |

329,439,73 ·   7,591,547,878

	Amount per Person in U.S.A.*
U.S. 2019 Gross Domestic Product of $21.3 Trillion Increase from 2013: 27.8%	**$64,655**
U.S. National Debt at $22.5 Trillion Increase from 2013: 28.4%	**$68,297**
Personal Citizen's Debt of $19.8 Trillion Increase from 2013: 18.6%	**$60,024**
U.S. Unfunded Liabilities of $176 Trillion **(Social Security, Medicare, Unfunded Government Liabilities)** Increase from 2013: 35.5%	**$534,240**
Debt per Person Increase from 2013: 31.2%	**$662,561**

* Based upon 329,439,738 people as of August 2019 (Source: U.S. Debt Clock, as retrieved from http://www.usdebtclock.org and U.S. Census Bureau Population Clock August 14, 2019.)

You can see United States National Debt rose dramatically since D'Apocalypse Now was written.

The National Debt has risen over 28%!

But, the most alarming statistics are showing U.S. Unfunded Liabilities (i.e. Politicians kicking the can down the road) increase by a whopping 35.5%, with the overall Debt per Person increasing by a huge 31.2%. Here are the figures and commentary following the "Debt per Person" table originally created December 2013:

US NATIONAL DEBT

$17,218,061,997,328

US Debt Clock.org

US NATIONAL DEBT	DEBT PER CITIZEN	DEBT PER TAXPAYER	US FEDERAL TAX REVENUE	INCOME TAX	PAYROLL TAX	CORPORATE TAX
$17,218,061,997,328	$54,307	$149,931	$2,823,738,361,424	$1,327,870,509,277	$961,354,320,961	$275,112,847,858

US FEDERAL SPENDING	US FEDERAL BUDGET DEFICIT	STATE REVENUE	STATE DEBT	LOCAL REVENUE	LOCAL DEBT
$3,481,467,462,561	$657,729,084,833	$1,549,635,764,188	$1,190,187,111,839	$1,056,772,243,045	$1,790,982,789,783

Largest Budget Items

MEDICARE/MEDICAID	SOCIAL SECURITY	DEFENSE/WARS	US GROSS DOMESTIC PRODUCT	TOTAL FEDERAL/STATE/LOCAL SPENDING	US POPULATION
$767,893,888,440	$811,346,452,136	$603,177,605,893	$16,003,093,796,276	$6,157,191,671,463	317,042,712

INCOME SECURITY	NET INTEREST ON DEBT	FEDERAL PENSIONS	GROSS DEBT TO GDP RATIO	REVENUE TO GDP RATIO	SPENDING TO GDP RATIO	US INCOME TAXPAYERS
$348,085,741,100	$254,919,512,995	$229,854,766,856	107.5924557%	35.3480403%	38.4751414%	114,838,792

US WORK FORCE: 143,388,298
NOT IN LABOR FORCE: 91,324,003

US TOTAL INTEREST • 2013	INTEREST PER CITIZEN	US TOTAL DEBT	TOTAL DEBT PER CITIZEN	TOTAL DEBT PER FAMILY	SAVINGS PER FAMILY
$2,625,509,298,647	$8,281	$60,183,374,264,117	$189,826	$752,564	$6,374

OFFICIAL UNEMPLOYED: 10,883,059

TOTAL PERSONAL DEBT	MORTGAGE DEBT	STUDENT LOAN DEBT	CREDIT CARD DEBT	PERSONAL DEBT PER CIT.
$16,082,118,174,078	$12,861,807,607,598	$1,051,912,824,162	$862,203,522,413	$50,725

ACTUAL UNEMPLOYED: 20,459,424

Money Creation

FEDERAL RESERVE MONETARY BASE	M2 MONEY SUPPLY	TREASURY SECURITIES	CURRENCY AND CREDIT DERIVATIVES
$3,714,257,673,412	$11,048,298,290,441	$628,115,127,617	$716,480,900,648,810

US RETIREES: 46,960,946
DISABLED (SSI): 14,298,826

Trade Numbers

US DEBT HELD BY FOREIGN COUNTRIES	US TRADE DEFICIT	US TRADE DEFICIT • CHINA	US IMPORTED OIL	IMPORTED OIL • OPEC
$5,783,656,919,524	$694,178,681,364	$320,973,174,237	$387,681,289,488	$147,651,834,956

LIVING IN POVERTY: 47,085,220
FOOD STAMP RECIPIENTS: 47,231,060

SMALL BUSINESS ASSETS	CORPORATION ASSETS	HOUSEHOLD ASSETS	TOTAL NATIONAL ASSETS	ASSETS PER CITIZEN
$8,647,676,813,533	$20,407,512,696,105	$77,217,363,299,079	$106,272,552,818,135	$335,194

STATE/LOCAL EMPLOYEES: 19,412,115

SOCIAL SECURITY LIABILITY	PRESCRIPTION DRUG LIABILITY	MEDICARE LIABILITY	US UNFUNDED LIABILITIES	LIABILITY PER TAXPAYER
$16,727,628,684,222	$22,131,939,485,962	$88,013,061,589,971	$126,872,629,882,260	$1,104,791

FEDERAL EMPLOYEES: 4,367,485

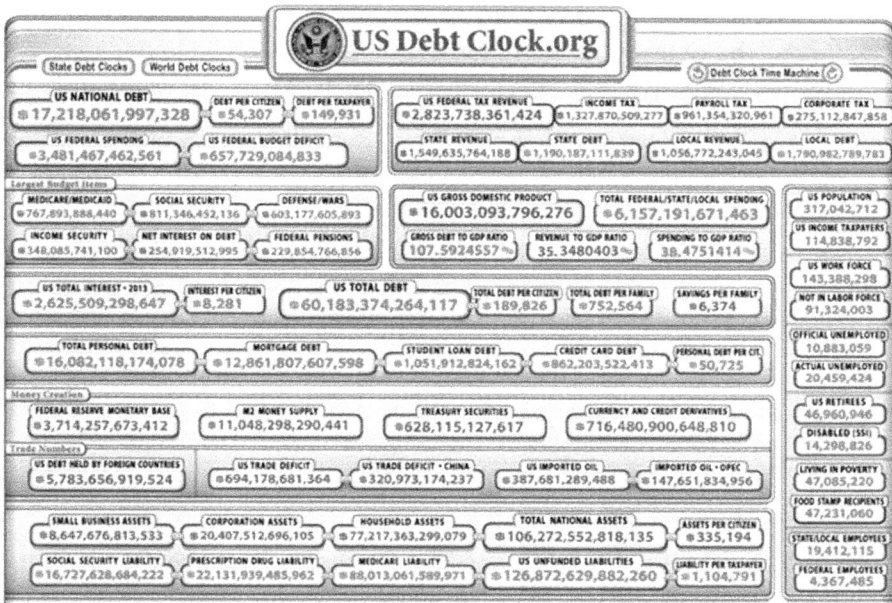

U.S Debt Clock December 7, 2013

	Amount per Person in U.S. A.*
U.S. 2013 Gross Domestic Product of $16.0 Trillion	$ 50,592
U.S. National Debt at $17.2 Trillion	$ 53,199
Personal Citizen's Debt of $16 Trillion	$ 50,592
U.S. Unfunded Liabilities of $126.9 Trillion	$ 401,259
Debt per Person	$ 505,050

* Based upon 316,254,000 people as of December 2013—see Chapter 7, "A Word on Unemployment," subsection "True Unemployment Picture." Above calculation ignores local debt. (Source: U.S. Debt Clock, as retrieved from http://www.usdebtclock.org).

"…Depending on how debt is dealt with will determine the resulting impact on the financial markets. When the problem is completely ignored and then combined with wild speculation and incredible leverage, the result is a poisonous cocktail which can completely wipe out any economy—especially if it is too highly leveraged." (Source: D'Apocalypse Now The Doomsday Cycle, pages 7-8)

To be clear, as the preceding evidence dictates, the only thing which has occurred under the Obama *and* Trump Administrations has been a very marked increase in spending and debt. Obama increased the debt by $8.6 Trillion (+74%) and Trump will increase the debt in his first term by $5.1 Trillion (+30%). Both of these actions yielded marginal increases in GDP, fueled by artificially low interest rates. George Bush was no choir boy, either. He increased the national debt by $5.8 Trillion of dollars (+101%) on his watch in order to get reelected and prop the markets up. This is the name of the game for all of them. They socialize the elite's losses, throw poor people out of homes, cause ingrained inflation, and low wages for the masses. When disaster strikes it will be because of their policies and conspiratorial coordination with the Fed.

When interest rates rise in earnest---Katy bar the door. If we use "Total US Interest Paid" expense figure in the 2019 Debt Clock and divide it by the total unfunded debt (Social Security, Medicare, plus U.S. Government Unfunded Liabilities) from the Debt Clock, one comes up with a 1.8057% interest rate (3,178,308,554,124 ÷ 176,012,458,580,656 = 1.8057%).

What do you think will happen if interest rates experience even a small rise to 3%? Even a modest rise in interest rates causes interest expense to blow up the federal budget. In fact at a 3% rate, the interest expense on the U.S. National Debt ($22,506,628,887,140) figure soars to an incredible $675,000,000,000. This does *not* include the interest on unfunded liabilities.

In other words, the bankers will be siphoning off from U.S. Taxpayers MORE money per year, than the entire U.S. Defense budget!!! The defense budget, using the Debt Clock figures in August 14, 2019 was $641,137,867,417.

As they say, "Something's gotta' give..."

Demacrash!

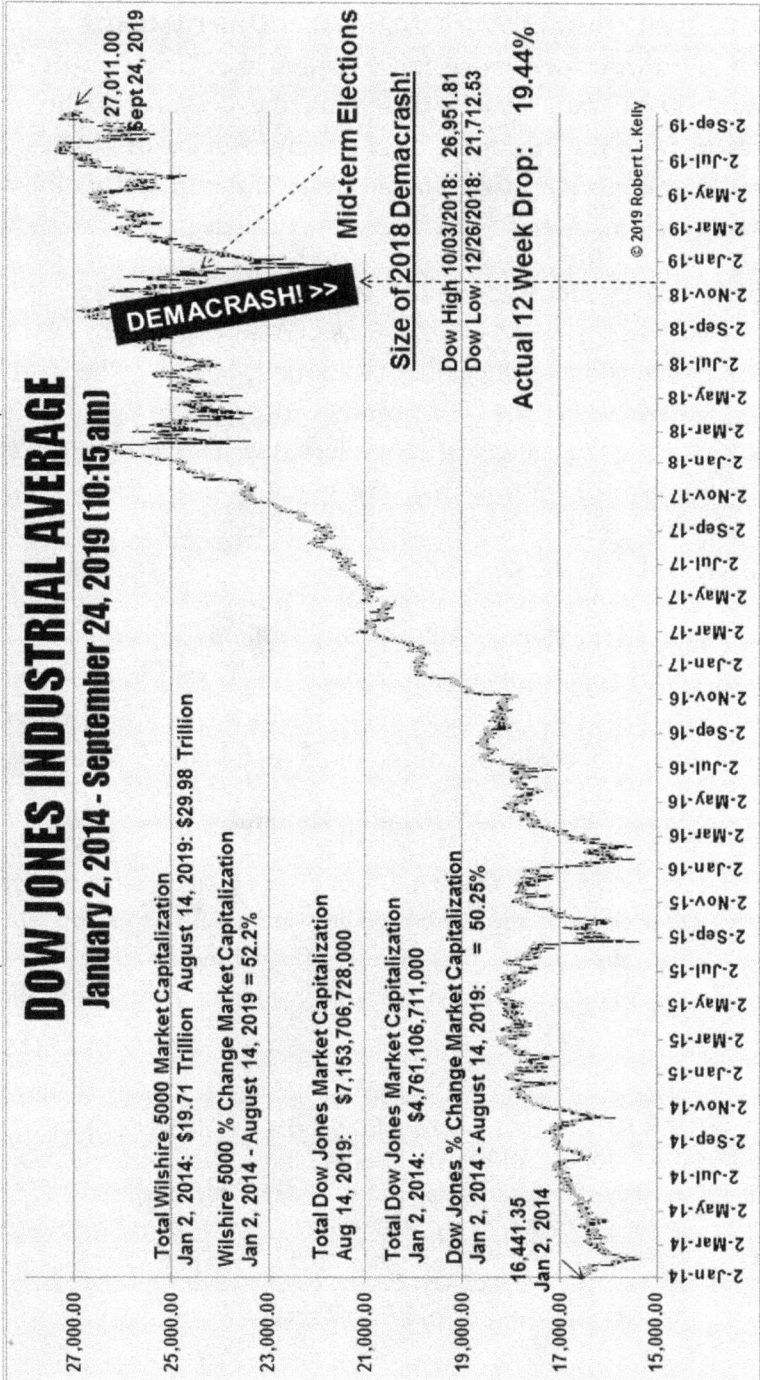

Size of 2018 Market Drop

DOW JONES INDUSTRIAL AVERAGE
January 2, 2014 - September 24, 2019 (10:15 am)

27,011.00
Sept 24, 2019

Mid-term Elections

DEMACRASH! >>

Size of 2018 Demacrash!

Dow High 10/03/2018: 26,951.81
Dow Low 12/26/2018: 21,712.53

Actual 12 Week Drop: 19.44%

Total Wilshire 5000 Market Capitalization
Jan 2, 2014: $19.71 Trillion August 14, 2019: $29.98 Trillion

Wilshire 5000 % Change Market Capitalization
Jan 2, 2014 - August 14, 2019 = 52.2%

Total Dow Jones Market Capitalization
Aug 14, 2019: $7,153,706,728,000

Total Dow Jones Market Capitalization
Jan 2, 2014: $4,761,106,711,000

Dow Jones % Change Market Capitalization
Jan 2, 2014 - August 14, 2019:   = 50.25%

16,441.35
Jan 2, 2014

© 2019 Robert L. Kelly

Demacrash!

REVERSE ROBIN HOOD ECONOMICS DEBT IMPACT

As the previous debt table for 2019 and the "Size of 2018 Market Drop" Dow chart shows, increasing the National Debt by $5.2 Trillion from the beginning of 2014 until August of 2019 (a 28.4% rise) bought an increase in market capitalization and wealth to the broad stock market of $10.2 Trillion (a 55% rise).

That's actually pretty good bang for the buck---if you are part of the 20% who own over 90% of all stocks. Alarmingly, only 1.1% of the people own 67% of all equities (see article, below). The wealth gap was worsened by the Fed significantly, due to their policy of socialism for the elite, with complete disregard for everyone else. This comparison by the way, *only* counts stock market riches. It doesn't include the wealth gained from real estate, collectibles, or the largest liquid market, debt securities.

The elite have reaped trillions and trillions through the Fed's surreptitious theft of money from the U.S. Taxpayer, as occurs each and every time the Federal Reserve issues a U.S. Treasury security, Federal Reserve credit, or engages in "Open Market Operations."

Stock Ownership Becoming Extremely Concentrated

"According to Goldman Sachs, stock ownership is extremely concentrated because of the growing wealth gap in the U.S., and thus the market's performance affects households making up the wealthiest 1% of Americans much more significantly than the other 99%.

'The wealthiest 0.1% and 1% of households now own about 17% and 50% of total household equities respectively, up significantly from 13% and 39% in the late 80s,' Daan Struyven, Goldman Sachs's chief economist said in a note earlier this week."
(Source: Yahoo News, "The richest 1% own 50% of stocks held by American households," by Heidi Chung, February 17, 2019 https://finance.yahoo.com/news/the-richest-1-own-50-of-stocks-held-by-american-households-150758595.html).

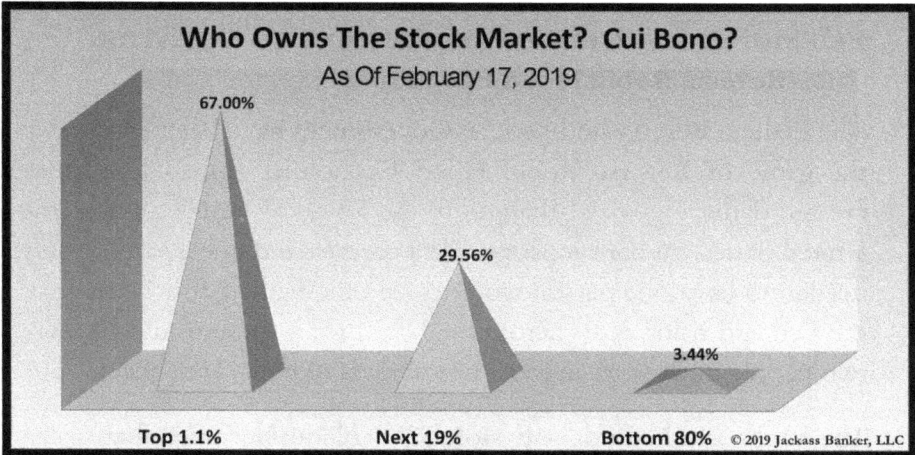

Who Owns The Stock Market? Cui Bono?
As Of February 17, 2019

67.00% — Top 1.1%
29.56% — Next 19%
3.44% — Bottom 80%

© 2019 Jackass Banker, LLC

2019 above, compares to 2010 below. 2010 was published in D'Apocalypse Now!---The Doomsday Cycle, page 201:

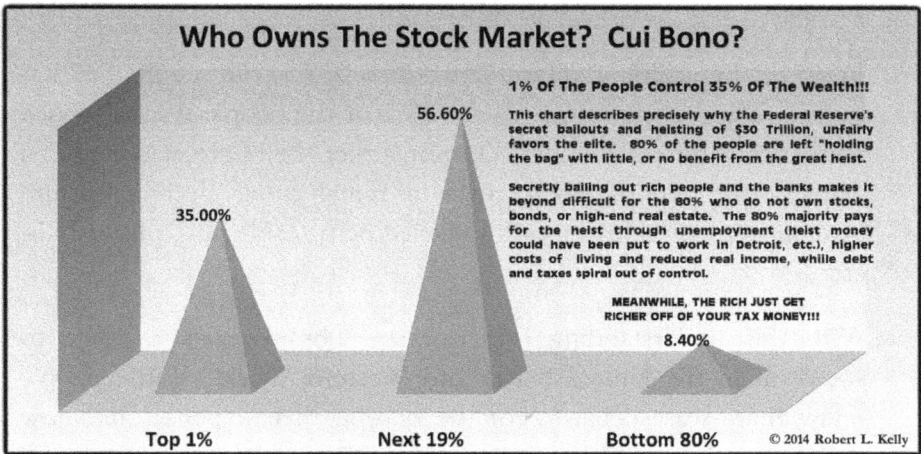

Who Owns The Stock Market? Cui Bono?

1% Of The People Control 35% Of The Wealth!!!

This chart describes precisely why the Federal Reserve's secret bailouts and heisting of $30 Trillion, unfairly favors the elite. 80% of the people are left "holding the bag" with little, or no benefit from the great heist.

Secretly bailing out rich people and the banks makes it beyond difficult for the 80% who do not own stocks, bonds, or high-end real estate. The 80% majority pays for the heist through unemployment (heist money could have been put to work in Detroit, etc.), higher costs of living and reduced real income, while debt and taxes spiral out of control.

MEANWHILE, THE RICH JUST GET RICHER OFF OF YOUR TAX MONEY!!!

56.60% — Next 19%
35.00% — Top 1%
8.40% — Bottom 80%

© 2014 Robert L. Kelly

These are dramatic wealth-transfer comparisons. They quickly demonstrate how the Federal Reserve's policy of "Reverse Robin Hood Economics" has worked out for the masses. Any grade-schooler can see it.

The rich are ripping off the middle class and poor in order to keep their wealth in tact. The evidence is as clear as day.

FED MONETIZES DEBT AWAY---LEADING TO INFLATION
---i.e. Reverse Robin Hood Economics

The Federal Reserve and Federal Government have been engaged in the game of Reverse Robin Hood Economics for so long, they created damaging social changes to the fabric of families across the United States. Where most people's parents and grandparents only needed to have one person work to feed the family, now because of the Fed and rising costs across the board for poor and middle class, two people must work in most households to make ends meet.

The banks and Fed not only stole $30 Trillion, but piled that stolen wealth onto the elite, and were complicit in destabilizing the nation with debt. All the while *both* Democrats and Republicans have done nothing to stop it. If the Democrats want to win---this is a key area to attack. The people have had enough.

From the preceding graphical comparisons, you can see the Fed has caused falling living standards for 80% of the people through stock market transferences alone. Do not forget they have also caused a tsunami-like tide of rising costs in rents, food, clothing, health insurance, medical, transportation, electricity, cable bills, phone bills, etc.

With this understanding one can see why there is a move to socialism in the United States and Western World. Little people know there was socialism for the rich, at their expense, and now they want their turn at the trough. Their reasoning is easy to understand.

Rich people stole all the money, and
the Fed used socialism for the rich to do it!

Thank Helicopter Ben Bernanke, Janet Yellen, Timothy Geitner, Jerome Powell, Allan Greenspan, Hank Paulson and a host of others for failed policies and destruction of the great middle class.

CHAPTER 3

THE TRUMP COUNTER PUNCH

WHAT THE PRESIDENT SHOULD DO TO WIN

Against these high stakes of a huge debt load, a potentially catastrophic rise in interest rates, the potential for an enormous drop in the stock market and poor economics for the masses (i.e. over 100 Million people of able working age, yet still unemployed), nine key suggestions are recommended to overcome the Democrats and seal their fate. These "9 Points," seen below, are succinctly summarized in this chapter. If the Republicans implement these ideas, they will soar to victory, but God help them if the Democrats move first and adopt them as policy objectives.

1) Prepare Against Stock Market Attacks
2) Keep the Peace at the Fed, but Shine Light
3) Do Not Use Gold to Back the U.S. Dollar
4) Fight Tooth and Nail Against Socialism
5) Reform Public Pension Funds Now
6) Direct Market Intervention for Farmers
7) Stop TV Networks From Creating Election-Time Blackouts
8) Use President's Working Group on Capital Markets
9) Declare a Debt Jubilee

Together, these nine ideas would make amends for the poor policies of the Federal Reserve and blast the economy forward. They also would rebuild our cities, preserve capitalism, assure President Trump's significant stamp on history and really keep America great.

Demacrash!

PREPARE AGAINST STOCK MARKET ATTACKS

1) Expect continued attacks on the stock market between now (September 2019) and the election in November 2020---and then again before the mid-terms in 2022 and the next Presidential election in 2024.

KEEP THE PEACE AT THE FED, BUT SHINE LIGHT ON THEM

2) Do not threaten to replace Jerome Powell. It will not help at this point. Instead, continue to press the Federal Reserve for continued loose monetary policy (i.e. low artificial

---

United States General Accounting Office

GAO

Testimony

Before the Committee on Banking, Finance and Urban Affairs
House of Representatives

Release on Delivery
Expected at
10:00 a.m. EDT
Wednesday
October 27, 1993

FEDERAL RESERVE SYSTEM AUDITS

Restrictions on GAO's Access

Statement of Charles A. Bowsher
Comptroller General of the United States

GAO AUTHORITY UNDER THE BANKING AGENCY
AUDIT ACT AND WORK AT THE FEDERAL RESERVE

We derive our Federal Reserve audit authority from the Federal Banking Agency Audit Act of 1978. This act was passed after we did a special congressionally mandated study of the supervisory activities of all of the federal bank regulatory agencies. Before the act, our work at the Federal Reserve was mainly limited to audits of the fiscal agent functions performed by Federal Reserve banks for the Department of the Treasury. We did this work under our authority to audit the Treasury.

Although the act significantly expanded our access to the Federal Reserve System and the other bank regulatory agencies, it precluded us from auditing activities related to monetary policy, foreign transactions, and the FOMC. The exact wording of the limitation is set out in Appendix 1. The act also prohibited us from disclosing certain information identifying open financial institutions and customers. Appendix 2 describes these prohibitions in greater detail.

(Source: U.S. General Accounting Office,
http://www.gao.gov/assets/110/105269.pdf)

52

"official" interest rates, quantitative easing and lower reserve requirements for banks, especially if the market tanks). To keep the Fed in line, the President should threaten the Fed with a complete audit. Bipartisan support exists for this. Use numerous available GAO reports which question the Fed's veil of secrecy around their actions to enrich the elite. This would likely force them to play ball. *Allow interest rates to rise* when real growth for the masses is accomplished by adopting the nine policy suggestions in this work.

As discussed, the race-baiting and outrageous lying one sees on TV has their root cause in the unequal and illegal distribution of wealth experienced by the country, ever since Ronald Reagan christened the birth of "The Plunge Protection Team." Using taxpayer money to prop up markets for purely political or financial gain for a super class of people should be ultimately outlawed. This hole in our system has permitted financial bubble after financial bubble to get blown, with the benefactors being the super wealthy.

The only way out of this predicament is to achieve real growth. The tax break the President pushed through was primarily a gift to corporations (although middle class workers were helped a little). Unfortunately, corporations have used the tax savings to buy back stocks, further enriching the top 1%, instead of reinvesting in growth and employment. It is very likely this investment of capital in stock buybacks will go up in smoke when the market drops like a rock when big Demacrash! hits in 2024. Their actions will prove to be a waste of trillions of dollars in unwisely spent capital.

Yes, after a crash the Fed can then "bid stocks back up," but this only seals the lucky fate of the wealthy. Costs will continue to rise out of sight for regular people. Wage stagnation and rampant real unemployment will continue to be the ingredients for one huge stick of social dynamite. Civil war will occur.

As we move to the third suggestion for the President, it is important to know why gold is *not* a good choice to back the U.S. Dollar, nor is it wise to put a "gold bug" on the Board of Governors of the Federal Reserve. The President has some smart people around him, but most of them likely don't know much about financial history.

Do Not Use Gold to Back the U.S. Dollar

3) This book forecasts in Chapter 6 how gold will sparkle as an investment in the years ahead. However, forcing it to back the U.S. Dollar, given our advanced economy, would be a disaster, economically speaking, for the general public.

This entire issue was painstakingly and historically documented in The $30 Trillion Heist---Follow The Money. The following passage reprinted from this book proves exactly *why* reverting to a gold standard causes *deflation* and *depression* for the masses. When gold is owned by the elite, their wealth increases with a gold standard while everyone else's wealth decreases. Back in the 1800's the Rothschilds owned the gold, and today it is the uber wealthy and central banks!

"Coinage Act" of 1873–Demonetizing Silver Cuts Money Supply Causes Massive Depression

In early 1873, both silver and gold were an acceptable form of currency and backing of paper currency in the United States, in accordance with our Constitution. At this time in history, England was the financial center of the world and controlled most of the supply of gold through the Rothschild family holdings. England did not have or possess, control of any significant amount of silver and neither did any other European nation. In the meantime, the U.S. was striking it rich with the discovery of silver mines out West. As a result, England and the Rothschilds (see subsection of this chapter, "Congressional Record 53rd Congress 1893, 1st Session," which follows, for Baron de Rothschild's own comments on the subject of silver) had *no interest* in America's "bimetallism," where both silver and gold were acceptable currencies.

In fact, if silver could be demonetized, they thought, there would be a rush for gold, effectively causing its value to rise, which would make the Rothschilds even wealthier-and to the advantage of England, as they controlled vast quantities of this precious metal.

1873 U.S. Silver Dollar
As retrieved from
http://coinauctionshelp.com/Seated_Liberty_Silver_Dollar.html#.UsHsa_RDuSp

Most believe the Rothschild's used every bit of their influence to ensure Congress passed the "Coinage Act" of 1873. This demonetized silver and caused the minting of silver dollars to halt. Gold became the only form of money to be coined.

By causing the demonetization of silver, there was an enormous contraction in the money supply—estimated at 4,000,000 ounces of silver and another 2,000,000 ounces of silver paper certificates. This amounted to an approximate 50% contraction in the supply of money and created one of the worst depressions, literally overnight, in American history, with at least one out of every three people unemployed.

American farmers, industry and the entire country received *less gold* when they sold the *same amount* of goods (see subsection of this chapter, "Congressional Record 53rd Congress 1893, 1st

Session," which follows, for a real-life history lesson on how North Dakota grain prices dropped enormously in terms of the price of gold during this period)—and England and the Rothschilds owned the most gold, allowing them to acquire assets, commodities and just about anything they wanted for a fraction of the price after the Coinage Act of 1873 was passed and silver could no longer be used as a currency. *By 1876, directly due to the massive contraction in the money supply, 1/3 of the U.S. population was unemployed.*

The Greenback was paper-currency issued by Abraham Lincoln backed by the promise to pay with the full faith and credit of the U.S. Government: "THIS NOTE IS A LEGAL TENDER FOR ALL DEBTS PUBLIC AND PRIVATE" (on the back of bill):

1880 $50 Dollar U.S. Note

The bill was printed in accordance with the Third Legal Tender of March 3, 1863. "Act of March 3 1863" is inscribed above Benjamin Franklin's Head on the front of the note. (Source: U.S. Bureau of Engraving, and Printing, credit to National Numismatic Collection at the Smithsonian Institution,
http://en.wikipedia.org/wiki/United_States_fifty-dollar_bill).

This was America printing DEBT-FREE MONEY! It was printed in the form of a United States Note (which bore no interest).

The following excerpts from the Congressional Record corroborate the description of events which led to the depression and which swept through the United States immediately after Congress passed the Coinage Act and demonetized silver. It provides clear testimony to the dark forces of the banking industry's involvement with this change to the law.

The Congressional Record focuses on the problems of the U.S. demonetizing silver and clearly shows the anger and angst of Senator Hansbrough of North Dakota. He has direct, written evidence of Baron de Rothschild's position and objective in ensuring silver was demonetized in the United States, making the Rothschild family's holdings of gold ever more valuable.

The Coinage Act was repealed in 1893, but the damage to the economy had already been done, with millions unemployed. The bankers, however, did get wealthier.

Demacrash!

Congressional Record 53rd Congress 1893, 1st Session

Congressional Record.

FIFTY-THIRD CONGRESS, FIRST SESSION.

Silver.

English Financial Tyranny and American Subserviency.

SPEECH
OF
HON. H. C. HANSBROUGH.
OF NORTH DAKOTA.

IN THE SENATE OF THE UNITED STATES,

Friday, September 22, 1893.

The Senate having under consideration the bill (H. R. 1) to repeal a part of an act, approved July 14, 1890, entitled "An act directing the purchase of silver bullion and the issue of Treasury notes thereon, and for other purposes"—

Mr. HANSBROUGH said:

Mr. PRESIDENT: The State whose people have honored me with their confidence does not produce an ounce of silver or of gold. Therefore I trust that what I shall say on the subject now under discussion will not be charged up as the utterance of one

for 1885 and 1886, that being a close approximation to the official figures for 1886, the only year in the period of 1885–1892 for which such figures exist. In the case of Asia Minor, Persia, and Syria blanks have been filled for 1886 and 1887, and in that of the Cape of Good Hope one has been filled for 1885 by the insertion of round-number figures bearing a reasonable relation to those for other years.

The reason for making these estimates, which it will be seen are in several cases rather arbitrary, is that by so doing it is made possible to obtain a total for each year for all the countries in the table, and that this total will not be appreciably affected, as regards its value for comparison with the totals for other years, by such a degree of error as there may be in the estimates for a few comparatively unimportant countries.

The following is the table:

Approximate statement of the world's wheat crop from 1885 to 1892, inclusive.

Countries.	1885.	1886.	1887.	1888.
	Bushels.	*Bushels.*	*Bushels.*	*Bushels.*
United States				
Ontario				
Manitoba				
Argentine Republic and Chile				
Austria				
Hungary				
Belgium				
Denmark				
France				
Germany				

Staples.	Value of an acre's product.					
	1866–1870.	1871–1875.	1876–1880.	1881–1885.	1886–1890.	1892.
Corn	$12.54	$11.30	$9.62	$10.25	$8.91	$8.55
Wheat	13.15	11.00	12.00	13.20	9.07	6.00
Oats	10.92	9.81	8.58	9.17	7.50	5.75
Hay	13.20	14.20	11.57	11.15	10.19	10.00
Cotton	26.01	26.53	17.65	15.63	13.84	10.65
Total	73.21	73.94	53.62	56.40	48.44	41.15
Average	15.64	15.19	11.68	11.28	9.89	8.15

Now, what has caused this fall in price in the face of underproduction and increased demands? Clearly and undeniably it is the increased purchasing power of gold that has caused it. It takes more pounds of wheat to buy a dollar in gold now than it did twenty years ago. That much must be conceded. The ratio of wheat to gold has grown larger year by year, just as the ratio of silver to gold has increased. It is a statistical and historical truth that the world's prices of wheat and cotton in this country have fallen with consistent regularity with the decline in the price of silver.

Now, let us for a moment inquire into the extent and importance of the silver industry on the American continent. The world's product of silver for the three years of 1890, 1891, and 1892 was in round numbers $555,000,000. Of this amount the western hemisphere produced $455,000,000, and all the other nations of the earth only $100,000,000. Is it any wonder that the Pan-American countries have a friendly side for silver when they produce nearly five-sixths of the world's total output? Silver is an American institution and is entitled to the strong protecting arm of the American people. Further disparagement of silver in this country at the behest of the great financial Moloch of Europe would be a national crime.

What is to follow the repeal of the Sherman law? Many of the friends of repeal say that the Government should buy gold to maintain the parity between our metallic moneys. The repeal press is now advocating such purchases, and that seems to be the policy which the Administration proposes to pursue. To do this a new issue of bonds would be necessary. The gold thus purchased would soon be taken from the Treasury by the money manipulators. Silver certificates and Treasury notes would be presented for redemption in gold then, as now, until the stock of the yellow metal became exhausted. It would then be necessary to issue more bonds to buy the gold back again.

The European nations that have thrown silver overboard did so under conditions far different from the conditions existing in this country. They do not produce silver. They have no great silver properties. When they eliminated silver as a money metal they did not strike down a great domestic industry. I would as willingly consent to vote for a measure to forbid the production of wheat in this country as to support a proposition to close the gold and silver mines of our great mountain region.

The banks there simply refused further advances to those of their customers who had been unfortunate in their investments. Pressed for immediate money, the holders of American securities were obliged to realize, and, as is well known everywhere, America is the only country that is doing business on a cash basis and is able to pay its debts as they fall due. Our bonds and stocks returned to us in large volume. Our gold went abroad in equally large proportions to pay for them. And in the midst of this situation the balance of trade turned against us.

These facts are historical. In them we find the germs, fully matured, of the late unusual depression. Then came the success in this country of a political party that has declared its purpose to turn prosperity's stream in the opposite direction. What followed is told in the record of failures and suspensions, the extent of which has never been equaled in so short a space of time in any country or under any circumstances.

It was at this critical moment that the enemies of silver, advocates of a single gold standard, opened their campaign against the Sherman law. They began to urge that distrust had arisen in Europe in respect to certain financial legislation in America. They asserted that foreign capitalists were fearful that we should adopt a policy antagonistic to our European creditors, and that the only way to obviate a terrible monetary disaster was to wipe from the statute books the last vestige of law recognizing silver as an element in our financial economy. The onslaught upon certain classes of our currency was shameful in the extreme. Patriotism, if they ever possessed it, vanished from the minds of the money-changers and bond-buyers. An assault was made upon the gold reserve in the United States Treasury.

The commercial yoke fastened to our necks in the time of George III was not more oppressive than is the financial harness we are now wearing by order of the house of Rothschild. We threw off the one by force of arms; we have it in our power to relieve ourselves of the other by legislation. The Hessians are with us now as they were then. They are clad in different raiment, it is true, but they are no less dangerous. Then they came in coat of mail; to-day they appear in purple and fine linen. What they attempted then by brute strength they are accomplishing now by the persuasive power of gold.

England is the bondholder of the world. Her people are creditors to the extent of $12,000,000,000. The debt is being paid day by day in a monetary medium the world's total volume of

That seems to have been conceded by the majority of the delegates in the conference. Baron de Rothschild, the English delegate to that conference, said explicitly and emphatically that England did not want bimetallism and would not adopt it. This is a matter of record. I shall quote from Mr. Rothschild further along in my remarks, in order that there may be no misunderstanding in respect to the position of England.

Now, where is the gold to come from when the United States enters the market as a purchaser? Mr. President, I have received letters recently from a friend of mine in London, a gentleman engaged in the business of bond-buying. He is well known to financiers on both sides of the water and his statements, upon a subject with which he is entirely familiar, may be relied upon. In his letters to me he says that the United States can not buy $50,000,000 of gold in all Europe; that the countries over there, which are on a gold basis, will not permit their gold to come here; that they can pay us much for it as we can pay, and will outbid us if necessary to keep it.

This describes the situation exactly. If we should buy Europe's gold, or any considerable portion of it, the financial stringency which we have been experiencing here would simply be transferred to the other side of the Atlantic Ocean. They will not let us have it except at an enormous premium. Financiers know this to be true and are getting ready to take part in the contest for gold that will inevitably follow the repeal of our silver legislation and the issue of gold bonds by this country. We would have an international scramble for gold instead of an international agreement in favor of silver.

which is less than one-third the total amount of the debt. In other words, the world owes England more than three times as much gold as there is gold in the world. English capitalists can, in thirty days, call for more gold than all the world would be justified in paying in ten years.

When England desires to squeeze a commercial rival all she has to do is to call in her gold. Thus the power is in her hands to force the business world into liquidation whenever it suits her purpose. Furthermore, a panic or business contraction in the United States makes a market for English goods. The closing of manufacturing institutions here, resulting in a smaller output of goods and wares, makes a market for cheap foreign products at good prices when business revives.

Author comment: **The Sherman Silver Purchase Act** of July 14, 1890, required the U.S. Government to purchase 4.5 Million ounces of silver per month, creating demand for the metal and increasing its popularity for use as a currency—a strategic plus for America, as it was discovering enormous quantities of silver across Pan-America at the time---much to the chagrin of England and the Rothschilds!

I have said that England would never consent to a bimetallic standard by international agreement or otherwise, and I have the proof here from the pen and the mouth of the man who dictates her financial policy. In a letter written to the governor of the Bank of England in November, 1886, Baron Alfred de Rothschild said:

I am strongly opposed to any radical change as regards the metallic circulation of Great Britain. * * * What would be the position of the Bank of England if bimetallism were to be introduced throughout Europe? I venture to think an extremely dangerous one.

Towards the close of this letter Mr. Rothschild made use of this significant language. I quote it literally:

As regards Germany, that country has also certainly a gold standard; but it would be difficult, if not impossible, to obtain any large amount of gold from Berlin or from any of the branches of the Imperial State bank.

Then, again, as to Italy, there is a large amount of gold stored away there; but, as in reality it does not see daylight, that country might as well not have departed from its paper currency.

Therefore, to sum up the situation in a few words, London being the center of the financial world, we have to be doubly careful to protect our stock of gold; but if bimetallism were introduced throughout Europe we should have much greater difficulty in doing so, and should be obliged to increase our stock of silver whether it suited us or not.

Gentlemen, I need hardly remind you that the stock of silver in the world is estimated at some thousands of millions, and if this conference were to break up without arriving at any definite result there would be a depreciation in the value of that commodity which it would be frightful to contemplate and out of which a monetary panic would ensue, the far-spreading effects of which it would be impossible to foretell.

The VICE-PRESIDENT. The Secretary will read as requested.

The Secretary read as follows:

According to good statisticians, in the year 1890 there were four billions of gold in the world as money, about four billions silver, and about four billions of paper, or twelve billions of money for the world's commerce, equal to $11 per capita for the world's inhabitants. If silver is demonetized it not only takes four billions of itself out as money, but also two billions of paper issued against it. In other words, it reduces the money of the world to six billions instead of twelve billions, as it is to-day, or a per capita of $5.50, equal to the per capita for the sixteenth century.

It will be readily admitted by the average business man of to-day that the per capita of money in the sixteenth century would not begin to do the business of the world at this period. I have before me a circular of January 23, based on and taken from the journals of the London Statistical Society, showing that from 1851 as the volume of currency (gold) increased the average price of all commodities increased. The volume of money and the highest average price of commodities culminated in 1873. In this year Germany demonetized silver and the scramble for gold commenced. From this time

473

the volume of money decreased and the average price of commodities decreased steadily, reaching a lower point in 1887 and 1892 than any other time since the circular was made up, 1841.

In view of these facts, who can deny that gold has appreciated? Gold is now coming back to this country, but under these conditions, namely, by our farmers selling their cotton and wheat at a discount of 20 per cent to 50 per cent, which shows the purchasing power of gold to be from 20 per cent to 50 per cent premium. Question: Must our farmers continue to supply the basis of replenishing our gold, or will the powers that be sell gold bonds and so lighten and distribute the burden of our gold importations until our supply of the precious metal is sufficient to restore confidence?

The Secretary read as follows:

One of Boston's ablest financiers, who has the reputation of doing his own thinking, and whose name is as widely known throughout the country as that of any other Bostonian, in fact one who is named in the daily press as a possible candidate for governor, says:

"I have no patience with this idea of reckoning everything from the commodity value of silver. It is mathematically clear to my mind that if all the silver in the world is to have its money valuation taken from it the value of the gold in the world will be doubled and the value of all property in the world must be cut in two, and a bushel of wheat or a bushel of corn will sell for one-half its former price. At the coining ratio there are only about equal amounts of gold and silver in the world, say a little under $4,000,000,000 of each; and each has cost the full measure of labor in production.

"The mistake that is made in the East here is to reckon everything from gold. It is like a man with a gold watch in one hand and a silver watch in the other, declaring that the silver watch is slow, when it may appear to him later that the gold watch is fast. Dry rot has been the ruin of the business world for twenty years, or since the demonetization of silver in 1873. It is either universal bankruptcy or the remonetization of silver.

(Source: The previous excerpts are from The United States Congressional Record, as retrieved from http://fraser.stlouisfed.org/docs/publications/mq53c/mq53c_v1sen_0030.pdf).

> After repeal of The Coinage Act in 1893, the bankers and the elite focused on how to create a central bank--- controlled by the elite families. It was passed in 1913 and is our Federal Reserve System of today…

Gold Standard Only Enriches Owners of Gold

As this brief several-page history lesson teaches, if a "gold standard" (or some derivative thereof) is used to back U.S. Currency, it will only *enrich* those who own gold. Everyone else will suffer deflation. As you have seen, this was documented in the U.S. Congressional minutes back in 1873. Farmer's, then one of the key economic pillars in society, went broke.

Today, the world's central banks, meaning the private banks that own them, control and own over 20% of the world's gold supply. If a move is undertaken to move to a gold standard, gold would skyrocket even more than what this writer expects to occur during the next several years. This kind of decision would only serve to enrich bankers and leave the population at the mercies of a deflationary depression.

The backbone of confidence in the United States and our country's strong Gross Domestic Product creates the strength of the U.S. Dollar, and the adaptation of its use worldwide. The U.S. Dollar is fundamentally strong IF the economy stays on track and our MILITARY is more powerful than anyone else's. These fundamental strengths, combined with confidence in our government, are the keys to a stable currency and a controllable gold price.

FIGHT TOOTH AND NAIL AGAINST SOCIALISTS (Especially, Stomp-Out Socialism for the Rich)

4) What is at stake is the direction of the country. Leftist Democrats want to take us in the direction of communism (not socialism). As educated people already know, heavily socialist states ultimately fail, or become relatively inferior contributors on the world stage. Make this one of the very most important campaign issues.

It is funny when Democrats point to "Sweden" as a great example of socialism. Ignorantly and confidently, leftist politicians state with confidence this is the direction the United States should go in.

Sweden's personal income tax rate for 2019 is 61.85%. They also have a societal disaster on their hands, as their liberal policies have allowed migrants to take control of their streets, with "no go" zones populating the nation and a flood of serious crimes has emerged. Many people argue liberal immigration policies destroyed what was once a peaceful country.

For the record, Swedes are a great, loving people. They make many things well, but they are not a serious economic growth story for most serious economists. In fact their GDP has dropped between 2011 and 2019. Volvos, as everyone knows, are generally overpriced and even an advanced manufacturing company like Nokia, from another socialistically-oriented country Finland, lost its competitive advantage. It got gobbled up by Microsoft for $7.2 Billion in 2013. Nokia continues to fail even with the backing of Microsoft.

There is a reason Silicon Valley, Silicon Alley, Seattle, Austin, Boston, Houston, L.A. and many other innovation centers exist in the United States: The United States holds the promise of tomorrow without it being stolen by government---although this is changing in California, Massachusetts, Illinois, New York and Seattle, as well as other parts of the country.

The basic problem is governments do not spend money wisely, at least not from the general public's perspective.

America rebelled against high taxes and will do so again. It is what America fought against when it battled the British and it is against our basic DNA as a country. Eventually, the pot will boil over and the time is approaching quickly.

Nothing beats capitalism to use resources the most efficiently and the most inventively. History has proven this. Innovation and low taxation are keys to a better life. We are far better off in a capitalistic system than a socialist or communist one, as long as the rules are the same for everyone. Unfortunately in America, they are not the same.

If you work for the government, or are one of its "leaders," then leaning "left" and being socialist means you can expect an unending gravy train of perks, healthcare and benefits (they receive generous pensions, while the rest of the population has to fund their own 401ks). As long as taxpayers allow it, the government bureaucracy will continue to grow.

Tick-Tock.

REFORM PUBLIC PENSIONS NOW

5) All public pension plans should be reviewed by voters not paid as consultants by the government, or universities. Avoid hiring "consultants" to make suggestions on the fairness of the pension plans in place.

Common sense dictates thieves have been at work, where unelected bureaucrats have voted themselves rich benefits at the collective voters' and student's expense.

Leave it in John and Jill Public's hands to determine the fairness of why government and university employees deserve free, egregiously rich pensions and health benefits, when everyone else is forced to fund their own.

The results would be stunning. Tuitions would drop, and unfunded liabilities which tower over the federal budget would be arrested, at least with respect to public pensions.

A long time ago clever government and university bureaucrats (the "deep state") figured out how to hire supposedly "independent" consultants to determine "appropriate" wage scales and pension levels. A consultant to the government (or university), is paid to justify egregiously rich benefits, creating an irreconcilable conflict of interest. All consultants need do is point to other universities or agencies and create a "pigeon" report. FYI---Consulting reports are called "pigeon reports" because we all know what pigeons leave when they fly away.

This practice of justifying massive salaries and pensions has become yet another form of legalized theft and no one in the judicial system has "pierced the veil" of fraud at the governmental and university levels. This needs fixing.

The pension fund crisis is going to be a beauty when its chickens come home to roost. This issue goes right back to the debt clock. It shows unfunded liabilities of $176 Trillion (about nine times the size of the U.S. GDP). Many projections indicate unfunded liabilities will grow to over $300 Trillion by 2030.

Congress' answer to the problem this year is to bail them out. This is the worst possible course of action for the broad population. Congress is bailing out the Pension Benefit Guarantee Corp---to the tune of up to $56 billion to cover insured liabilities. Socializing the losses of greedy people seems to be a cancer run amok in the United States.

It is outrageous the taxpayers are paying for the poor decisions of employers, unions, universities, government agencies and elected-government officials.

Washington Post: Should taxpayer money be used to bail out key pension plans?

"Today, the government considers about 10% of the 1,400 plans 'at risk.' The projected unfunded liabilities, in turn, could swamp the PBGC, whose multiemployer insurance fund had $2.3 billion in cash to cover insured liabilities of $56.2 billion as of Sept. 30, 2018…At the heart of the issue: the mammoth Teamsters' Central States Pension Fund. With an unfunded liability exceeding $20 billion, it is on course for collapse by 2025…" (Source: "Omaha World-Herald", April 29, 2019 https://www.omaha.com/opinion/washington-post-should-taxpayer-money-be-used-to-bail-out/article_4aca5529-94fc-56a1-bc85-e1780472dd36.html).

The simple question common people ask is: "*Since government and university employees didn't used to make more money than the private sector, why are they receiving free pensions and big paychecks today?*"

Collectively, these coddled groups of government and university employees have orchestrated an outrageous abuse of power, and manipulated the system for their own enrichment. Tackling government and university pensions won't solve the enormous pension problems at the state and city levels (where soulless leaders have voted themselves fat paychecks), but it is a start.

The President should not touch Social Security or Medicare, however.

Whatever President commits to serious pension reform and puts this power into the people's hands will go down in history as one of the very best. What better way to break up the historically corrupt Teamsters than by letting it fail?

DIRECT MARKET INTERVENTION FOR FARMERS

6) Start purchasing agricultural production in the open market and **buy up** wheat, corn, soybeans, pork and beef. Send the food to Africa for the poor, in exchange for mineral and port rights, and cause a good deed to happen. This will also help farmers and the entire agricultural industry. Granting farmers billions of dollars in direct aid, as the President has, is fine---but, there is nothing like *price* pressure on China to prod them into making a good trade deal.

Even if Japan really does buy up the excess soybeans via its new trade agreement, the President should keep the pressure on China through direct intervention. Too many political players are obviously trying to delay him to see if he wins reelection. This is hurting his agenda.

Finally, socializing agriculture with direct-aid handouts makes for lazy farmers. Use the free market to make a positive change for agriculture. It is long overdue.

STOP CABLE NETWORKS FROM CREATING ELECTION-TIME "BLACKOUTS" FOR FOX & AMERICA ONE

7) On August 15, 2019 in the morning, the author was tuning in to Bloomberg, CNBC, CNN and Fox. The author lives in Manhattan in New York City.

At 7:23 am, when the television tuned to Fox Networks to see what the curvy couch had to say, a big-blue screen indicated there were "technical difficulties" and the Fox channel wasn't operational. It also provided a phone number to call (833-831-3141). The network in question was Spectrum, owned by Charter Communications, and is based in Stamford, Connecticut.

After dialing the phone number, the author reached some random tech company. The number on the TV screen provided by Spectrum was incorrect. Intrigued, the author looked up Spectrum's phone number, dialed it, and waited to speak with an operator.

Curious as to why only one channel out of about 400 didn't work and still waiting for Spectrum customer service, the author searched on Google's search engine for cable network's which were down and not operating that day.

This is what was discovered:

Fox News outage map

Recent reports mostly originate from: Philadelphia, New York City, Poughkeepsie, Brooklyn, Catonsville, Columbia, The Bronx, Bradenton, Detroit, and Lynchburg.

| Fox News outage chart |

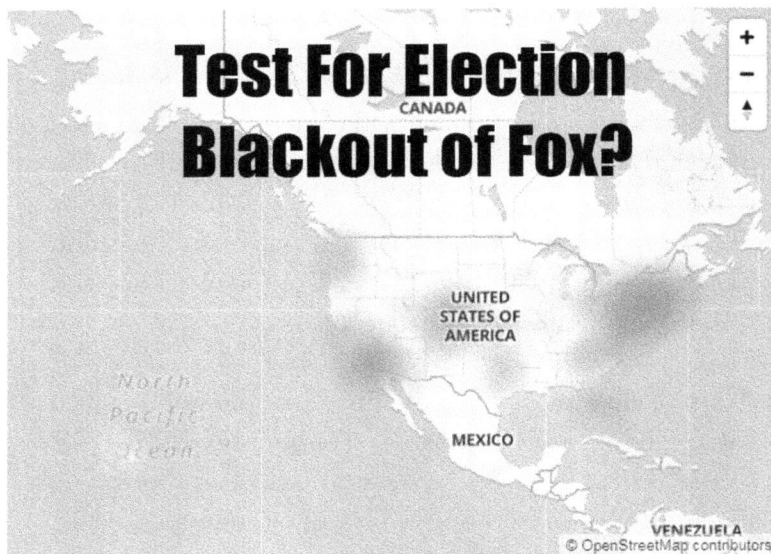

Test For Election Blackout of Fox?

CANADA

UNITED STATES OF AMERICA

North Pacific Ocean

MEXICO

VENEZUELA
© OpenStreetMap contributors

Fox News is a cable TV channel and news site.

7:23 am
August 15, 2019

Credit: https://downdetector.com/status/fox-news/map

FOX NEWS channel

One look at this outage map, and red flags went up. (Headline is author's commentary). Once finally connected, the author complained and indicated it was highly suspicious *only* the Fox News Network was "down" across the country.

The author's advice to the President is: do not believe in coincidences---and pay attention to outage tests like this.

Solution: Reestablish Fairness Doctrine at the FCC

"The fairness doctrine of the United States Federal Communications Commission (FCC), introduced in 1949, was a policy that required the holders of broadcast licenses both to present controversial issues of public importance and to do so in a manner that was—in the FCC's view—honest, equitable, and balanced. The FCC eliminated the policy in 1987 and removed the rule that implemented the policy from the Federal Register in August 2011...

...Stations were given wide latitude as to how to provide contrasting views: It could be done through news segments, public affairs shows, or editorials. The doctrine did not require equal time for opposing views but required that contrasting viewpoints be presented. The demise of this FCC rule has been considered by some to be a contributing factor for the rising level of party polarization in the United States...

...The fairness doctrine is not the same as the equal-time rule. The fairness doctrine deals with discussion of controversial issues, while the equal-time rule deals only with political candidates." (Source: Wikipedia, https://en.wikipedia.org/wiki/FCC_fairness_doctrine).

As documented meticulously in The $30 Trillion Heist---Follow The Money!, Volume II of The Federal Reserve Trilogy in Chapter 14, page 167, the major media companies are controlled by the big banks and their allies.

The Murdoch's have control of Fox, hence their ability to speak somewhat differently than every other liberal channel on television. However, the Murdoch family's enormous stake in

Walt Disney, after its acquisition of Fox assets, puts them clearly in the hands of the bankers---as Disney has $16-$17 Billion in debt on its books after the merger.

Tucker Carlson said it exactly right on his show one evening this past summer. The real issue facing our country is income inequality (Tucker didn't say the banks and the Fed stole $30 Trillion, but he might if he read the author's books) and what better way to keep people's minds off this issue than by stirring the pot, name-calling, race-baiting and spewing hatred toward Trump?

To most honest people, it is easy to see how the broadcasters twist the truth to fit their agenda, making them a propaganda tool for the elite.

This has caused a shutdown of alternative thought in the United States and the problem isn't isolated to television. It is also critical to address the growing problem of censorship on the Internet.

Google, Microsoft, Yahoo, Bing, Snapchat, Instagram, Google Mail, You Tube, Apple, etc. need to be held accountable for the free-flow of thought over their networks---without operator, algorithm, or other interference. Internet usage is at least equivalent to broadcast usage today, and should be treated as such by the federal government.

Today, for example, when people search on Google, the only news they see is the "news" Google wants you to see---with the political spin on the news they want you to absorb.

These are not conspiracy theories, they are concrete truths---the tech industry is reminiscent of a fiefdom, split up between Kings and Queens, where what they say goes---and woe to the person who disagrees with them.

Stopping this Nazi-like propaganda system at the major television networks and technology companies is mission critical to the survival of a truly democratic republic.

One of the President's greatest strengths is to be out in the open with the people. This creates great confidence for him and his Administration, because he is not only reaching 20,000 people in the stadium, he is reaching millions on television and online.

If TV and/or certain internet portals are taken away through mysterious "technical problems" during the fall of 2020 especially, it could have a major impact on the President's ability to get his message out.

Forewarned, is forearmed, Mr. President.

EMERGENCY FED/MARKET MEASURES
USE PRESIDENT'S WORKING GROUP ON CAPITAL MARKETS

8) If the previous points discussed (and specifically regarding the Federal Reserve) do not stop the bleeding in the markets, the President should task Steve Mnuchin with making the markets fly higher. He has the machinery in place to do it---so make him do it. Since the budget deal, there is no real limit on spending for the federal government during the next two years.

Personally, the author abhors this suggestion, but this is about winning the election. The alternative, due to the biggest financial bubble ever blown in history, is disaster for everyone. If President Trump can complete the trade deals with Europe, USMCA (i.e. U.S. Mexico Canada), Japan, the U.K. and China and force the Fed to play ball---markets will skyrocket…and real growth will return, possibly bailing us all out of the debt mess we are in. Signed trade agreements need to be ratified by Congress before they are "completed."

This leads us to the most important thing to do for the people.

DECLARE A DEBT JUBILEE---USURY, HEART OF THE PROBLEM

9) The Bible and history provide insight into how to solve the enormous debt problem we face, today. In The Bible, God ordered Israel to declare a Debt Jubilee every 7 years. All debts were forgiven.

The President, through Executive Order and action, should borrow from the wisdom of The Bible and combine it with a plan similar to what Julius Caesar implemented when ancient Rome had an economic crisis in his time. Not many people know this, but Caesar also faced a tough situation caused by too much debt.

The system God admonishes against is a system which builds too much debt and leverage. This can cause a man, a woman, or an entire society to be enslaved to a master, other than God.

Usury and debt are bad. Everyone knows they create social evil. They take providers' time away from families and away from worshipping God. Today, most families must have both parents work all the time just to make ends meet. This means millions of households have nobody at home watching the children.

God wanted to set men and women free and created this earth to be their bread basket. With a little work, people could feed, clothe and house their families, inexpensively. God did not want His people to become debt slaves.

In Deuteronomy, God gave orders to ensure a debt jubilee (debt forgiveness) occurred every 7 years for the Jewish people. In later verses, He tells them it is still fine to charge foreigners for their debt---and the debt jubilee was only for the nation of Israel. Somehow, this wisdom is calling out to us, today:

> ### The Year for Canceling Debts
> "[1]At the end of every seven years you must cancel debts. [2]This is how it is to be done: Every creditor shall cancel any loan they have made to a fellow Israelite. They shall not require payment from anyone among their own people, because the Lord's time for canceling debts has been proclaimed."
> (Source: The Bible, Deuteronomy 15: 1-2 New International Version).

Jubilee Specific Courses of Action
Allow Deduction of Historic Interest Payments from Principal

People in the bottom 80% of the population, most impacted by the Fed's Reverse Robin Hood Economics, should have their historic interest payments credited toward a direct reduction in the principal they owe the banks---on *any loan*.

A) CREDIT CARDS/HIGH INTEREST LOANS

Ever since the banks legally made payoffs to Congress in a form of bribery to end the usury protection laws, consumers have been paying for it. The siphoning off of buying power from the U.S. household is a big reason why two heads of family must work today. Typically before in our country's history, they didn't have to.

The money paid out to credit card companies and lenders is astronomical. The following is what our Founding Fathers envisioned for people before bankers started lobbying Congress for higher interest rates:

Abbreviated History Abolishing Usury Laws

Early 18thCentury American colonies adopt usury laws, setting the interest cap at 8%.

After 1776 All of the States in the Union adopt a general usury. Most states set the interest limit at 6%.

1916 A Uniform Small Loan Law allows specially-licensed lenders to charge higher interest rates—up to 36%—in return for adhering to strict standards of lending.

1945-1979 All states adopt special loan laws that cap interest at higher than the general usury rate—at 36%—but cap it nevertheless. (Source of "Abbreviated History Abolishing Usury Laws" above: Democratic Underground, https://www.democraticunderground.com/discuss/duboard.php?az=view_all&address=114x58796).

Finally, along the way, from 1990-2005, banks also lobbied Congress to make it harder for a person to declare bankruptcy and start over (for student loans). (Source: Cappex.com, https://www.cappex.com/articles/money/history-of-bankrupty-dischange-for-student-loans)

2019 Impact of High Interest Rates on Credit Cards

The difference between 36% interest and 8% (8% was the originally allowed interest rate, historically) = 24%.

The existing credit card debt in 2019 on August 14 (per the U.S. Debt Clock, as shown previously) is $1,071,354,050,379.

24% x $1,071,354,050,379 = $257,124,972,091 in maximum interest expense to consumers.

$1,071,354,050,379 in total credit card debt equates to <u>$6,657 per cardholder</u> (per the U.S. Debt Clock).

Author note: the Federal Reserve was started in 1913 and it is no coincidence rates charged to the people went up dramatically a few short years after it was formed---to 36%.

B) Grant Interest Payment Credits on Mortgages

Provide individuals with an interest rate credit and reduction of their principal owed on existing mortgages to mortgage holders going back to 2003. Repayments of interest directly to the 40 Million people who were thrown out of their homes during the credit crisis must be part of this plan. The banks have been convicted of crimes in court, though not one banker was sent to jail; yet 40 million people were thrown out on the streets when the banks foreclosed. Justice must be served through payment to these unfortunate people.

No lawyers should be involved. Get the money directly to the people and keep the middle men out of it.

By helping mortgage holders in the lower 80% of society (not the upper 20%) society would be strengthened. It would also make it a better place to live for the super-rich and middle class, while righting another wrong.

If implemented, this would create the country's greatest real estate boom in history and strengthen the economic might of the country for decades to come.

Increased buying power would be formidable.

Unfortunately, this also means some banks and mortgage companies might get in financial trouble. If and when a bank or mortgage company can't pay the credits owed to the consumer, then the group of consumers should become creditors of that bank. To avoid years of ridiculously complicated litigation (and lawyers taking 1/3 of the proceeds), banks and their existing shareholders would make the affected consumers 25% owners of the bank, or mortgage company, with the elimination of preference shares (i.e. preferred stock) in those companies.

This solution would create dilution for existing shareholders of the financial institutions affected, but it would not destroy the system of finance we have in our country. This system is a strength long term, but it is being abused by the people who own and run it.

Collectively, these financial reforms would go a long way to correcting the wrongs of the banks and the Fed during the credit crisis.

Rationale for the Jubilee

The banks, as proven in The $30 Trillion Heist---Scene Of The Crime? took $30 Trillion in stolen money from the American people. By declaring a "Debt Jubilee," this gives some money back to the people, without destroying the nation---or the banks.

A Debt Jubilee for the nation would cause the stock market to hit 50,000, but it would also light the economy on fire. It would also aggressively reduce the National Debt, provided Congress doesn't spend the windfall. A Debt Jubilee should translate into lower tax rates as GDP growth would explode upward and government tax revenues would soar.

Let's face it; the banks have had their way with us for far too long. The people making investments in the banks who don't see change in the air will lose money. Those who are wise will change their asset allocation models.

Just like Julius Caesar, we need a law, or Executive Order and Action, allowing the bottom 80% of Americans to apply their past interest payments against the principal owed.

The story of how Julius Caesar saved Rome and the empire from an economic and real estate meltdown and depression is fascinating. It is well worth reading. It is brief and is reprinted as follows:

Demacrash!

Julius Caesar

When Caesar was rising to power in 59 BC when he was first elected to consul in the first Triumvirate, the Triumvirate included himself, Pompey (the foremost military commander to whom Caesar reported and to whom Caesar's daughter was married, also in 59 BC) and Crassus (a wealthy financier). As most are taught in their history lessons, the Roman Senate at the time was well known for its extreme corruption and jealousy, making it difficult for any one person to become a supreme emperor.

"Die ErmordungCäsars**"**

Caesar surrounded in the Senate, being murdered. By Karl von Piloty(1826–1886) , painted in 1865. The painting is located in the Lower Saxony State Museum (Source: Wikipedia, as retrieved from http://en.wikipedia.org/wiki/Julius_caesar).

During the next ten years or so, Caesar consolidated his power through a series of brilliant military and administrative actions which ultimately made him Rome's supreme dictator, effectively neutralizing the Senate. Militarily, his actions included the invasion of and conquering of Gaul (modern-day France) and Great Britain, WITHOUT the consent of the Senate, and ultimately destroyed Pompey's army in Spain.

By law, the armies of Rome were supposed to remain above the Rubicon River in Northern Italy, which divided Italy from Gaul. The Roman Senate had created this artificial barrier to ensure they had the run of the country, without military interference. When Caesar crossed the Rubicon on January 10, 49 BC, it is said he spoke the famous words:

"Alea iacta est, translated as "The die is cast."

Throughout this period, Rome was having a Civil War with many economic problems. Caesar had to pay his legions and the Senate was taxing the "citizens" to death---forcing many of Rome's citizens to flee the high taxation rate. This led to Caesar passing laws limiting HOW LONG a person could stay away from Rome (3 years) and he made other edicts which encouraged scientists and teachers of the liberal arts to live in Rome by FREEING them of taxes imposed by the city. This attracted the most brilliant minds of the day to live in Rome and encouraged others to live there, also, causing the tax base to rise. He took other actions, causing Rome to give public land away to 20,000 freemen, provided they had three children, or more, and to his soldiers. Caesar knew tax receipts increase if land was cultivated and population growth was increasing.

He also knew his soldiers would fight for him if they were rewarded for loyalty. Julius Caesar also *reduced* the number of people receiving corn at the expense of the public (i.e., welfare) from 320,000 to 150,000 people and he invoked taxes on the importation of foreign goods.

In one of his bravest decisions, which helped most people throughout the land, dramatically improved the economy and perhaps in itself, ended the civil war, **Caesar issued a decree regarding the repayment of debt on property.** Because of the civil war and high taxes, the economy was in rough shape and property prices had dropped precipitously, causing mortgages to be "under water." **The lenders wanted to foreclose and the borrowers wanted to be let off the hook.** Because of Caesar's appeal to the people, most thought Caesar would decree the debt would be forgiven and borrowers would not have to repay the lenders. Caesar did not suggest this.

Instead, Caesar had the properties assessed at their respective values prior to the civil war--when the values were much higher--and allowed all interest payments to be deducted from those revised values, whether the borrower paid it back in money, *or in a personal bond. This was a personal obligation of the borrower, without the need for a banks' approval!* This allowed people who had no money to STAY IN THEIR HOMES and refinance in a manageable manner! This action reduced the debt by approximately 1/4th.

XLII. Eighty thousand citizens having been distributed into foreign colonies,[1] he enacted, in order to stop the drain on the population, that no freeman of the city above twenty, and under forty, years of age, who was not in the military service, should absent himself from Italy for more than three years at a time; that no senator's son should go abroad, unless in the retinue of some high officer; and as to those whose pursuit was tending flocks and herds, that no less than a third of the number of their shepherds free-born should be youths. He likewise made all those who practised physic in Rome, and all teachers of the liberal arts, free of the city, in order to fix them in it, and induce others to settle there. With respect to debts, he disappointed the expectation which was generally entertained, that they would be totally cancelled; and ordered that the debtors should satisfy their creditors, according to the valuation of their estates, at the rate at which they were purchased before the commencement of the civil war; deducting from the debt what had been paid for interest either in money or by bonds; by virtue of which provision about a fourth part of the debt was lost. He dissolved all the guilds, except such as were of ancient foundation. Crimes were punished with greater severity; and the rich being more easily induced to commit them because they were only liable to banishment, without the forfeiture of their property, he stripped murderers, as Cicero observes, of their whole estates, and other offenders of one half.

XLIII. He was extremely assiduous and strict in the ad ministration of justice. He expelled from the senate such members as were convicted of bribery; and he dissolved the marriage of a man of prætorian rank, who had married a lady two days after her divorce from a former husband, although there was no suspicion that they had been guilty of any illicit connection. He imposed duties on the importation of foreign goods. The use of litters for travelling, purple robes, and jewels, he permitted only to persons of a certain age and station, and on particular days. He enforced a rigid execution of the sumptuary laws; placing officers about the markets, to seize upon all meats exposed to sale contrary to the rules, and bring them to him; sometimes sending his lictors and soldiers to

[1] Principally Carthage and Corinth.

Excerpt from The Lives of the Twelve Caesars see source information at end of this section.

What a difference it would have made if any politician worth his or her salt, stood up against the bankers and declared---"All homeowners can write their own bond at the Federal Reserve Borrowing rate (it has been at nearly zero percent for the banks all throughout the crisis) and self-finance not only their home, but also enjoy an immediate credit against their owed principal with the deduction of all historically made interest payments!"

Collectively, Caesar's actions helped him end the civil war, enthroned him to power and set Rome off in the right direction, which led to the establishment of the Roman Empire, formed Europe and allowed Rome to rule for centuries. The history books tell us of the jealousy and fear Senators had of Caesar disbanding the Senate. As we know, Caesar was murdered. It would be interesting to know if the murderers, Gaius Cassius Longinus and Marcus Junius Brutus, were also lenders who had to forgive ¼ of the debts owed to them!

(Source: The Lives of the Twelve Caesars, by C. Suetonius Tranquillus, translated by Alexander Thompson, revised and corrected by T. Forester, Esq. A.M., pages 14, 15, 18, 19, 24, 25, 28, 29, published by George Bell & Sons, Covent Garden, London 1890, http://files.libertyfund.org/files/1888/1235_Bk.pdf and http://www.ultimatebiblereferencelibrary.com/The_Twelve_Caesars_of_the_1st_Ce ntrury_-_Suetonius.pdf).

Author comment: this work, "The Lives of the Twelve Caesars" as of 1500 A.D. (after the printing press was invented) no less than 18 editions were printed, with the world's scholars artfully and carefully translating each and every word. This work is held in very high regard by academics, worldwide, with respect to Caesar and his lasting legacy.

CHAPTER 4

MARKET FORECAST

Against the backdrop of all-out political war between the Democrats and Republicans, investors want to know---what should I do?

Chapters 1, 2 and 3 laid the foundation which instructs each party how to try and seize power.

In the belief we are fighting a battle between Principalities and Powers, the author's opinion is to pay attention to who is in power and what they are doing to the money. Knowing this information allows a sophisticated market matrix and economic outlook to be created, which can be amazingly accurate, as demonstrated by forecasts in D'Apocalypse Now!

Just like that work, Demacrash!, provides readers with specific, actionable recommendations in the chapters ahead. Detailed forecasts cover the broad market, stocks, bonds, commodities and foreign exchange over the next five years. The final chapter is what to expect in 2025+.

Each chapter doesn't mess around, either. The author's style is to shoot straight and not waffle. While there will certainly be incorrect stock picks and perhaps a forecast may be wrong, this book provides recommendations, specifically, as to what to own---or what to sell. There is no gray, or the mincing of words. The author leaves you with his preferences for black and white investment decisions.

****

JUST MAKE SURE YOU SPEAK WITH A FINANCIAL ADVISER BEFORE MAKING ANY INVESTMENTS. NEITHER THE AUTHOR, NOR JACKASS BANKER, LLC ARE FINANCIAL ADVISERS AND DO NOT PROVIDE INDIVIDUAL FINANCIAL ADVICE. FURTHERMORE, MANY OF THE RECOMMENDATIONS IN THIS BOOK ARE EXTREMELY AGGRESSIVE AND MAY NOT BE SUITABLE FOR ALL READERS. IN FACT, MANY OF THE RECOMMENDATIONS ARE LIKELY ONLY SUITABLE FOR A FEW SOPHISTICATED, QUALIFIED PEOPLE! TO TAKE FULL ADVANTAGE OF THE RECOMMENDATIONS AND TO PROPERLY ASSESS THEIR RISK CHARACTERISTICS, READERS SHOULD BE PROFESSIONALLY CAPABLE IN THE USE OF FUTURES, OPTIONS AND TRADING IN HIGHLY VOLATILE MARKETS. THIS INCLUDES FUTURES, COMMODITIES, DEBT, EQUITIES, FOREIGN EXCHANGE AND OTHER LEVERAGED MARKETS.

****

The author is amazed at the thousands of books sold by financial writers who get it wrong---each and every time---yet they are still being interviewed by Fox, Bloomberg and CNBC. Truth wins out, eventually---so the author keeps writing, forecasting and putting on free educational trading demonstrations.

This book's investment-related chapters include market sectors designed for the most sophisticated investor with charts, graphs and stop/loss points, as well as for the beginner (with direct stock choices to buy and sell, or approach with caution).

Naturally, sophisticated investors may choose futures, options, over-the-counter transactions, commodities, as well as Blackpool and foreign exchange markets to potentially take advantage of this author's next set of prognostications. A careful read of the book will uncover great opportunities in leveraged markets particularly, because the upcoming market changes may be spectacular.

The investment chapters are also designed to be short and to the point. People interested in markets can quickly grasp the author's viewpoint, specific recommendations, and run with them---or not. There are visual aids to help in making quick decisions.

The good news for investors is *no matter* what happens, you increase your chances of doing extremely well if you follow the forecasts and recommendations in this book---particularly if the author's global forecasts are correct.

As one of the most insightful, brilliant and published forecasts of the last decade, D'Apocalypse Now! was right on the mark, both strategically and tactically speaking, from an investor's point of view. The probability of being correct in its key forecasts tallies to either nearly 1000:1 odds or 100:1 odds, depending on how you calculate it. The bottom line is the list of fulfilled forecasts is impressive. The author is not aware of another individual who published a book, years in advance of market action, stuck to his forecast---and then been proven correct.

The author doesn't claim to have a pipeline to God, either. The author's books are the result of paying attention to thousands of facts, cyclic behavioral factors and a zeal for understanding international and national events which impact economies. A good computer helps, also.

As a result, not many analysts in the world can come close to the author's success rate in matters of financial forecasting.

And please remember, most people thought the author was *crazy* when he said the Dow would rise to between 22,000 and 37,000 when he wrote the original forecast in 2013 for <u>The Federal Reserve Trilogy</u>.

Without stating the obvious, the author points this success rate out because his hard work is driven by the desire to help others prepare for what he believes is likely to come our way and ultimately, it is not good news. Those who heeded his advice have steered clear of danger and the author prays, once again, God will bless his work.

While the financial books he has written always make recommendations for change to avoid the potential collapse of the system due to excessive debt and spending, a person would be foolish to not see the debt tsunami heading our way. The debt apocalypse is on track to financially wipe out millions of people, worldwide.

This book doesn't concentrate on derivatives which are a key focus of Volumes I, II and III of <u>The Federal Reserve Trilogy</u>. However, the reader should know derivatives have *grown* in size since 2014, and the banks have successfully erased the stigma of using them since the near calamity of the credit crisis from 2007-2010.

Anything can go wrong in the derivatives market, and don't believe what you hear from the Federal Reserve about how the banks have enough money to withstand economic trouble ahead. It isn't true.

In fact, at the first sign of real trouble, banks are now empowered to seize *your* deposits and assets under their control----this includes checking, savings, brokerage, futures, commodities and foreign exchange accounts. We have all seen how countries in crisis limit withdrawals of money. From China, to Cypress, Argentina, Venezuela and now showing up in Europe, countries are scared; they know an even bigger monetary crisis is on the horizon.

The recommendations in this book will not be worthwhile unless you have a plan to get your assets out of the banks' hands and into a private security vault. The author promises you will sleep way better at night if you make this change as soon as possible.

It is scary to think about the subject of monetary collapse and most people set it aside for another day to worry about later, thinking:

> *"Well, I can't do anything about it, so I*
> *should just go about my daily routine and ignore it."*

This is normal human behavior. But, sometimes in history, rewards are granted to the prepared. Those who are wise and see the signs, can take action and survive---even thrive.

BROAD MARKET FORECAST

Economically speaking, the world is in a nose dive. This is expected to go on until the beginning of 2020. The general stock market has a very good chance of experiencing a drop in the fall of 2019 and into the beginning of 2020. However, given the enormity of the bull market blast-off about to be launched, it is possible no serious correction occurs and the market just takes off.

The odds favor a bottom, possibly a spike low on October 25, 2019 (+/-4 days) is possible, with a weak rally thereafter, and a possible retest (or slightly lower Dow print of another -5%) of that low in January 2020. Don't be too cute in trying to buy "the low," because this market is getting ready to **blastoff** for the stars, and you don't want to miss that first move up---even if you buy early.

Sometimes being too cute causes you to miss the boat, and no one wants to miss the rocket ship launch coming up in equities markets in the United States. Like a rocket ship---the initial launch in the equities market for the last leg of the bull market may be powerful.

FORECAST BUILT ON FOUNDATION OF D'APOCALYPSE NOW!

While the previous forecast in 2014 from D'Apocalypse Now! predicted the market would have a target range of 22,000-37,000, the actual time it took to hit that range took a couple of years longer than what was frankly expected.

The overall scheme, however, was and is right on target.

The fact remains <u>D'Apocalypse Now!</u>, being a book with a limited shelf life, gave the specific instruction to be out of the markets by May 2015, allowing investors to be saved from a terrifyingly fast drop in August of that year, which saw a vicious 10% decline in the stock market over just a few weeks. This scared the Fed and the Obama Administration so much, they bought the market, literally, and shot it higher, in yet another bailout of supposedly free markets. With the move back up, the target of 22,000-37,000 was ready to go.

Readers who adhered to that book's advice, have done very well for themselves and have been able to sleep at night.

The book also provided target objectives of how high the Dow Jones Industrial Average would rise. The words and text written in <u>D'Apocalypse Now!</u> as published in February 2014 on page 314 are:

> *"Adjusting this number for inflation, with the 75.08 factor, calculates to an equivalent 2013 Dow Jones Year-end number, adjusted for GDP growth and inflation…of 58,652.53.*
>
> *Remarkably, both these numbers, '28,617.75' (which is right in the middle of our target range…) and '58,652.53' are potential target areas from a technical perspective."*

The author's charts continue to hold investor merit pointing toward continued upside action, with periods of healthy and scary declines along the way. The high for the bull market thus far, was on July 16, 2019 with the Dow Jones Industrial Average reaching 27,398.68. This was nearly in the middle of Mr. Kelly's original target range.

Demacrash!

An interesting look at the market's financial history beginning at the uncanny "Exit" signal of May 2015 issued nearly a year-and-a-half *earlier,* follows:

STOCK MARKET PERFORMANCE IN MID-2015

"The DJIA closed at a record 18,312 on May 19, 2015[8] before slowly falling to a low of 17,504 and then partially recovering to its secondary closing peak of 18,102 on July 16.[9][10]

The stock market slowly slid thereafter, reaching a low of 17,403. The NASDAQ Composite peaked on July 17, 2015 at 5,219. Apple Inc.'s stock peaked at $133.00 on February 20, 2015, reached $132.37 on July 20, 2015 and slid to $105 by August 21, 2015.[11]

THE DOWNTURN

Stock market performance between August 18, 2015 and August 21, 2015

On August 18, 2015, the Dow Jones Industrial Average (DJIA) fell 33 points. On August 19, 2015, it lost 0.8% and on August 20, 2015, it lost 2.1%. A steep selloff then occurred on August 21, 2015, when the DJIA fell 531 points (3.12%), bringing the 3-day loss to 1,300 points.[11]

STOCK MARKET PERFORMANCE ON MONDAY, AUGUST 24, 2015

On Monday, August 24, world stock markets were down substantially, wiping out all gains made in 2015, with interlinked drops in commodities such as oil, which hit a six-year price low, copper, and most of Asian currencies, but the Japanese Yen, losing value against the United States Dollar. With the stock market plunge on Monday, an estimated ten trillion dollars had been wiped off the books on global markets since June 3.[12]

The 8% drop in China on August 24 was termed "Black Monday" by the Chinese state media.[13] The term gained wide usage in the next 48 hours.[14]

In India, the Sensex recorded its biggest single-day fall of 1,624.51 points on August 24, ending the day down 5.94%. Indian investors registered losses worth over ₹7 lakh crore (₹7 trillion (US$100 billion)).[15]

In Europe, the main stock markets dropped at least 3% on August 24. The FTSE lost -4.4% (£78bn) but upon opening on August 25, shot up 116 points (1.97%).[16][17]

The DJIA opened 1,000 points lower on August 24, but gained nearly half of it back in the first 30 minutes. The New York Times used the term "upheaval" to describe the market situation.[18] It remained down 588 points at the close of trading. Hedge funds, which, for the most part, had long positions on the eve of the downturn, suffered substantial losses as stocks such as Apple, Citigroup, Facebook and Amazon lost value.[19]"   (Source: https://en.wikipedia.org/wiki/2015%E2%80%9316_stock_market_selloff

8. Mahmudova, Anora; Mozee, Carla (May 19, 2015). "Dow ekes out another record close". Marketwatch.
9. "Dow Jones values historical and today". CNNMoney.
10. "Dow Jones Industrial Average interactive chart". Bloomberg L.P.
11. Li, Shan; Chang, Andrea; Dave, Paresh (August 21, 2015). "Stock market suffers worst one-day drop since 2008". Los Angeles Times.
12. Popper, Nathaniel; Gough, Neil (August 23, 2015). "Global Stocks Tumble Further Amid Doubts About China". New York Times. Retrieved August 24, 2015.
13. "markets lose ground amid 'Black Monday' for Shanghai index". Washington Post. Retrieved August 24, 2015.
14. "Black Monday and Tumble Tuesday: How China reacted". BBC. Retrieved August 24, 2015.
15. Mehra, Puja; Ninan, Oommen A. "Sensex crashes 1,624 points; investors lose over ₹7 lakh cr". Chennai, India: The Hindu. Retrieved August 24, 2015.
16. Exchange, London Stock (August 25, 2015). "London Stock Exchange - FTSE Values". London Stock Exchange. London Stock Exchange. Retrieved August 25, 2015.
17. Smout, Alistair (August 21, 2015). "European stocks suffer worst 1-day fall in nearly 4 years". Reuters. Retrieved August 24, 2015.
18. Popper, Nathaniel; Gough, Neil (August 23, 2015). "Stocks Off Sharply as Market Upheaval Grows". New York Times. Retrieved August 24, 2015.

19. Alexandra Stevenson and Matthew Goldstein (August 24, 2015). "A Stock Market Rout in a Month That Hedge Funds Would Sooner Forget". The New York Times. Retrieved August 25, 2015. Hedge funds went into the sell-off bullish, with $1.5 trillion in long positions — bets that stocks will rise in price..."

Readers who adhered to the author's advice and **EXITED** by the end of May 2015 saved themselves a 15.69% haircut when the markets got slaughtered worldwide in August of that year. In the last week of May of 2015, the Dow had a high of 18,229.75 and the low for the sell-off came on August 24, 2015 at 15,370.33. The actual high for that particular cycle was seen the week of May 18, 2015 where the Dow hit 18,351.59.

There is a good history lesson here: When the markets tank, politicians (and the Fed) panic.

CURRENT SITUATION
Unfortunately, like Pavlov's dog, they continue to pump money into the market. When things are bad, they artificially inflate and support stocks, bonds and other assets, rather than permit the free market to eliminate bubbles and companies which have been poorly managed. Their strategy will work until confidence evaporates, which will occur very likely starting in 2024. At this time, decades of abuse shall be wrung out of the markets, virtually overnight.

The Obama Administration's policies created much slower growth than what otherwise might have been expected between 2014 and 2016 particularly, given the doubling of the national debt on that Administration's watch. In fairness, before Obama, George Bush also mismanaged the deficit and piled on debt to the tune of trillions of dollars---all in an effort to bail out the banks and the economy, instead of allowing the free market to work (see page 46 for details).

Both of these Administrations during the credit crisis could have simply protected homeowners and depositors---and punished the investors and shareholders who made poor investment decisions in the banks and related mortgage obligations. Others would have been standing in line to takeover JP Morgan Chase, Goldman Sachs, Citibank, etc. But, the Fed and the politicians chose to bail out the elite---members of their club---and this is why we are still in the brutal conundrum we are in today. The debt keeps piling up and every politician continues to kick the problem down the road, hoping the Ponzi scheme doesn't end on their watch.

Identifying when this game of musical chairs stops, and everyone scrambles for a seat, is the key. The time is getting very close, and just like a game of musical chairs, the music sounds the most lively and joyful, just before it is abruptly shut off.

When Donald J. Trump got elected and his purported growth-oriented policies were put in place, the market kicked in and soared. The problem is, the growth in the equity markets and economy has come at the expense of expanding debt, accompanied by burdensome government spending deficits.

Unfortunately, the tax-cut Trump envisioned for the people was poorly administered and planned by RINOs (Republican in Name Only) in Congress, and his staff. The plan had zero incentive for companies to invest the tax savings they received back into the economy---except as it might pertain to the top 20% of Americans who own the stock market. The results were predicable. The corporations primarily used the tax savings to buy back their own stocks, which drove up earnings per share and allowed stock prices to rise. This allowed executives to reap huge bonuses.

This is one of the reasons President Trump is dealing with a great deal of hatred from many in the republic.

The best way out is to permit real growth to occur. However, to accurately measure growth, the government needs to stop publishing phony jobs numbers out of the Bureau of Labor. These figures damage all Presidential Administration's credibility, as there are still over 100 million people unemployed of working age, who are willing and able to work, yet they cannot find jobs.

If President Trump were to implement some, or all of the policy recommendations this book makes in Chapter 3, especially and including a "Debt Jubilee," real job growth would soar and the deficit would shrink. It is difficult to think how high GDP might rise in such a scenario.

Obviously, with this book predicting a grim future for 2025+, it is betting the Trump Administration does not implement meaningful reforms, but will try to rely on "easy money" and trade deals to boost markets. Ultimately, these factors and the debt cycle create a massive economic debacle brought on by rising interest rates (in the free, "non-pegged" markets), along with the prospect of socialism/communist policies on the horizon.

The President would undoubtedly like to implement real reforms, but the Deep State and powers within the banking establishment are clearly against him. It is rumored President Trump thinks of himself as Andrew Jackson reborn; but, given the enormity of the debt problem, the prospect of rising interest rates, and failing pensions, instead, he might be well served to use the wisdom of Abraham Lincoln over the next several years.

A very small history lesson is instructive. When Lincoln was losing the Civil War, he created the "Greenback." President Trump should recreate the Greenback, and do away with borrowing using Treasury securities bearing interest to meet the federal government's spending needs. This idea is covered and documented in detail in The Federal Reserve Trilogy.

> "On February 25, 1862, Congress passed the first Legal Tender Act, which authorized the issuance of $150 million in United States Notes." (Source: Brands, H. W. (2011). Greenback Planet: How the Dollar Conquered the World and Threatened

Civilization as We Know It. University of Texas Press, p. 12; Wikipedia
https://en.wikipedia.org/wiki/Greenback_(1860s_money).

Many will say this strategy and tactic to defeat debt would be highly inflationary---but, again, they don't know history. After Lincoln printed Greenbacks via the Legal Tender Act, the dollar did depreciate against gold during the Civil War. After the country recovered, it rallied back to an even exchange rate with gold.

> "In 1862, the greenback declined against gold until by December gold was at a 29% premium. By spring of 1863 the greenback declined further, to 152 against 100 dollars in gold. However, after the Union victory at Gettysburg the greenback recovered to 131 dollars to 100 in gold. In 1864 it declined again as Grant was making little progress against Lee who held strong in Richmond throughout most of the war. The greenback's low point came in July of that year: 258 greenbacks equal to 100 gold. When the war ended in April 1865 the greenback made another remarkable recovery to 150.[9] The recovery began when Congress limited the total issue of greenback dollars to $450 million. The greenbacks rose in value until December 1878, when they became on par with gold. Greenbacks from thereon became freely convertible into gold.[10]   (Source: ibid [10] Zarlenga, S. (2002). The Lost Science of Money (pp. 460-463). Valatie, NY: American Monetary Institute).

A switch to an interest-free Greenback would be magic for the people and reduce the government deficit significantly. It also would be no more inflationary than what the Fed plans and what it currently does. Today, the Fed monetizes the debt through surreptitious Caribbean Shell Corporations, and willing allies around the world, via debt guarantees. The huge difference under a Greenback plan is everyone benefits---not just the elite.

As has been shown in this book, the Dow Jones Industrial Average has little direct impact on over 80% of Americans. A rising Dow makes rich people richer, but most of the people with regular 401Ks are not meaningfully impacted by the Fed's outrageous, skullduggerous shenanigans to drive markets higher.

Predicting the exact "end" of when the politicians' spending and easy-money policies of the Fed begin to fail is a challenge. This is why most pundits get it wrong. Most of the time, they leave out key facts and basically parrot what they hear from various investment gurus. They do little or no, original research (e.g. unlike the author's original work on the $30 Trillion secretly stolen from the American people by the banks and the Federal Reserve) for their analysis.

However, given the reliance on facts and not wishful thinking, the ultimate Dow Jones Industrial Average price targets provided in 2014 by the author, along with a blow-off top potential in the years ahead to over 50,000 on the Dow, are still tracking for potential achievement. D'Apocalypse Now!---The Doomsday Cycle forecasts have provided eerily accurate prognostications of where the Dow and the markets are heading.

Boldly forecasting multiple years in advance is not an exact science; however, the research and thinking behind the methodology of the author provides astute investors with guide posts which should help keep them out of trouble, and potentially allow good returns on their investments.

Warning: While wildly bullish from 2020-2024, this book expects big trouble ahead. The following is the forecast for the Dow Jones Industrial Average from 2019-2032. Astute investors please pay close attention to the TIMING suggestions in the author's various forecasts, because not all markets are the same. The suggestions are designed to try and help investors know when to buy, sell, hedge and bail out of the markets---given the author's perspective. The stakes are going to be enormous.

All forecasts and comments in this book are strictly the author's opinion. All investors and traders should seek advice from their appropriate financial advisers before making any investments. The opinions and forecasts in this book are published in accordance with the 5th Amendment of the United States Constitution.

The interim high, to date, for this bull market was July 16, 2019 at 27,398.68. A "Fake-Out" new high (with a target level at 27,719) may be seen before a fall correction begins. However, the market will decide where it tops, and it could even go even higher before turning down. See "Dow Jones Industrial Average Trump Victory Forecast" chart which follows.

Is Mr. Kelly Really a Great Forecaster?

Readers who do not know Mr. Kelly's work or previous books may like to know about the trading demonstrations Mr. Kelly performed at the Jackass Banker website during the last two years, along with other warnings and predictions he made.

Education is important to the author, and it is why he conducted two different theoretical trading demonstrations, which managed diversified portfolios over 60- and 90-day periods yielding:

- +124% from March 26, 2019-June 24, 2019
- +84% from April 10, 2018-June 5, 2018

These figures are not annualized, and there were many trades tracked in the portfolios. The two demonstrations were free to the public, and were provided as an educational service at the website. The first demonstration lasted for approximately 60 days in 2018 and the second one lasted for 90 days in 2019.

The effort witnessed the real-time construction of theoretical portfolios and the execution of theoretical trades within them during the trading periods. 2019, for example, witnessed 70 different trades executed over ninety days. Detailed, time-stamped proof of the theoretical trades can be viewed at http://www.jackassbanker.com/2019-model-portfolio.

Demacrash!

Dow Jones Industrial Average 1998-2032
Trump Victory Forecast

Debt Apocalypse!

Wave 4: Democrats will use every trick in the book to crush markets in the fall of 2019 and into 2020. Trump & team effectively fights back. A veritable battle of the ages is about to unfold.

All Dow/S&P long entries should be purchased in December 2019. If Trump weakly implements stimulus vis-a-vis this book's recommendations, a collapse could happen into the elections (i.e. November 2020).

Gold & Commodity stocks are treated differently than regular equities.

The Democrats, if they lose in 2020, will leave no stone left unturned to crash the markets prior to 2024 elections. A Democrat victory in either 2020, or 2024, assures a crash scenario.

The forecast in this chart assumes a Trump VICTORY in 2024. If he loses---the big "CRASH" forecast to begin in 2024 will arrive early---catalyzed by the 2020 election defeat of Trump, and the socialist agenda of the Democrats being implemented during the last half of the 2020s!

27,719 ? Fake-Out High?

27,398.68
DJIA High
July 16, 2019

DEMACRASH!

Commodity Storm!
Inflation & Fast
Rising Interest Rates!

Wave 5: If Dow breaks above 37,000-it's likely heading between 40,000 and 50,000! Time frame for rally to end will be late 2023 - May, 2024.

Sell all positions no later than December 31, 2023!

2024 STOCK MARKET COLLAPSE LIKELY!
Lasts 6-8 years
Target low below 10,000 in 2032!

DEMACRASH! >>>

9,900 ?
Multi-Year
Low

Wave 4: Fast, Sharp, Scary Drop in Fall of 2019! This correction will look like the Bull Market is over!

Don't be fooled!! The greatest rally of a lifetime is coming!! Target low for a late fall 2019 drop is 20,000 to 23,300. If the Dow hits 22,500, execute the buy on Dow & related stocks in this book. The coming "up" cycle will be huge-one of the biggest price moves ever seen.

If the Dow doesn't hit 22,500...buy equity DJIA/Big Cap positions when Dow rises over 28,000!

© 2019 Robert L. Kelly
www.jackassbanker.com

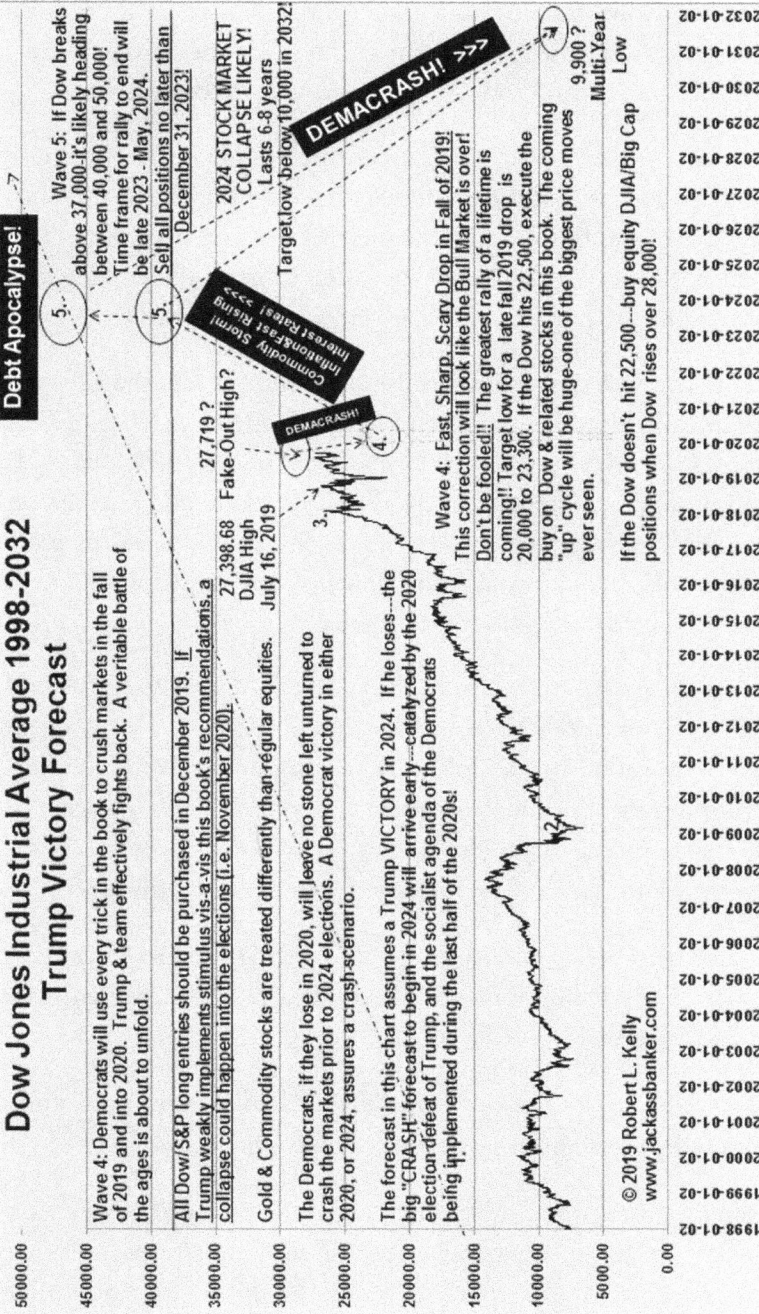

Dow Jones Industrial Average
Trump Victory Forecast

95

Demacrash!

The model portfolio traded the Turkish Lira. It made a theoretical fortune by going long the U.S. Dollar vs. shorting the Turkish Lira---all "time-stamped" with Google Ads to prove date & time:

Finally, a copy of the "final" profit from the 90-day trading exercise in 2019 follows, as captured in the Model Portfolio financial statement used each day to track profitability of the portfolio. The theoretical portfolio rose 124% in the three months the trading was demonstrated to the public. 2018's is out on the website.

A careful analysis of the trading in the portfolio reveals the use of a wide breadth of different markets to achieve results, relying heavily on Jackass Banker's proprietary Black Box trading platform. It provides buy and sell signals on 44 different markets. Futures on equities, debt, commodities and foreign exchange transactions were used extensively making portfolio changes, as appropriate, with Black Box guidance and market intelligence.

The 2019 portfolio started with $1,000,000 on March 26, 2019 and was worth a theoretical $2,248,457 on June 24, 2019---a 124% gain in 90 days. $1,000,000 was an arbitrary starting point, as the markets traded were among the most liquid in the world. This means the Black Box and trading capability of Mr. Kelly could theoretically be useful for very large portfolios, including sovereign wealth funds.

2018 results were also published on the Jackass Banker website. That 60-day performance saw the theoretical portfolio increase by 84%. It also began with a theoretical $1,000,000.

Good forecasting relies not only on the ability to academically study and research, but also the ability to know *how and what to trade.*

There aren't many hedge funds which place the kinds of ads Jackass Banker does (i.e. bold, amazingly specific and mostly correct), or publishes the kind of information found in this book and other books written by the author.

Theoretical   **Results**

Turtle Trading Data Array — Model Portfolio
24-Jun-19 — Portfolio Started March 26, 2019

Futures Market	Corn	Lean Hogs	Soybeans	Orange Juice	S&P 500 emini ES	Silver	Nasdaq 100 (NQ)	Gold	Crude Oil	Coffee
Underlying Contract	5,000	42,000	5,000	15,000	$50	5,000	$20	100	1,000	37,500
Exchange	CME	CME	CME	CME	CME	CME	CME	CME	CME	CME
Contract Mo.	Jul-19	Aug-19	Jul-19	Jul-19	Sep-19	Jul-19	Sep-19	Aug-19	Aug-19	Sep-19
Long/Short	Long	Long	Long	Long	Short	Long	Short	Long	Long	Long
# Contracts/Unit @ 2%	74	44	64	72	12	54	20	38	11	48
Unit Average Cost	4.4700	0.7420	9.2025	0.9900	2951.50	15.4250	7757.5000	1423.30	57.7500	1.0370
Unit 1 Entry Price										
Unit 2 Entry Price										
Unit 3 Entry Price										
Unit 4 Entry Price										
Total # Contracts	0	0	0	0	0	0	0	0	0	0
Market Price	4.4700	0.7420	9.2025	0.9900	2951.50	15.4250	7757.5000	1,423.30	57.7500	1.0370
Value Underlying Contract	$22,350	$31,164	$46,013	$14,850	$147,575	$5,000	$155,150	$142,330	$57,750	$37,500
Market Value of Contracts										
Less Opening Commission & Fees*										
Unrealized Gain/(Loss) Open Positions										
Less Closing Commission & Fees*										
Realized Gain/Loss Closed Positions/Column	$895,081	-$269,501	$139,144	-$37,344	-$132,104	$435,066	-$232,587	$329,987	$293,174	-$172,459
Initial Margin/Contract	968	1,485	2,057	1,056	6,930	3,630	8,360	3,740	3,400	1,005
Initial Margin										
Maintenance Margin/Contr.	880	1,350	1,870	960	6,300	3,300	7,600	3,400	3,100	915
Minimum Maintenance Required										

Total Unrealized Profit/(Loss)—Open Positions: $ -
Total Realized Profit/(Loss)—Closed Position: $ 1,248,457

* Assumes an estimate of $3.00/contract for each side (i.e. when you buy and when you sell)—includes the estimate for exchange & NFA fees.

Summary Account Information

	Model Portfolio	
	Start Date	Today's Date
Initial Capital April 10, 2018	1,000,000	3/26/2019 — 6/24/2019
Unrealized Profit/Loss Open Positions	-	
% Unrealized Gain/Loss	0.05%	
Account Balance After Unrealized P/L	1,000,000	
Account Balance After Realized P/L	2,248,457	
Total Margin Deposits	-	
Total Maintenance Deposits Required/Cont.	29,675	
Additional Margin Deposits	(29,675)	
Realized Profit/(Loss) Closed Positions	1,248,457	
% Realized Profit/(Loss)	124.85%	ANNUALIZED % PROFIT (LOSS) UNREALIZED + REALIZED
% Realized + Unrealized Profit/(Loss)	124.85%	THE BELOW IS A HIGHLY VOLATILE NUMBER GIVEN THE SHORT PERIOD OF TRADING TO DATE
Total Profit/(Loss) Open & Closed Positions	$ 1,248,457	506.32%

www.jackassbanker.com

You can see these figures enlarged on the Jackass Banker web site (link to the trading blog: http://jackassbanker.com/2019-model-portfolio/).

As a reader "FYI" Mr. Kelly personally invented and scripted the Black Box trading model used in managing the portfolios.

Finally, Jackass Banker published and time-stamped via Google Ads, several advertisements in 2019 warning people of certain events about to unfold in the markets. http://jackassbanker.com/2019-model-portfolio/our-google-ads/

The following are three of those advertisements:

This first Google advertisement was run 3 days before the summer 2019 high was registered on the Dow, which hit a high of 27,398.68 on July 16, 2019. By August 15, 2019 the Dow interim low had hit 25,339.60---a drop of 7.1% in a month's time.

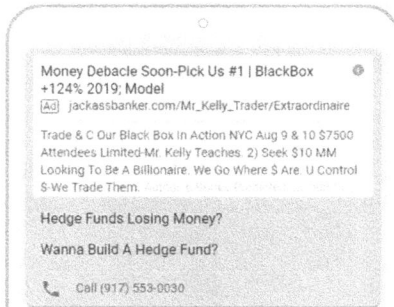

Google Ad Run July 12, 2019 (see below)

DON'T SAY WE DIDN'T WARN YOU!

Ad	Version ↓	Approval status	Ad group	Policy details
Money Debacle Soon-Pick Us #1	BlackBox +12 4% 2019; Model	Portfolio +84% 2018 1) Lear... jackassbanker.com/Mr_Kelly_Trader/Extraordin aire Trade & C Our Black Box In Action NYC Aug 9 & 10 $7500 Attendees Limited-Mr. Kelly Teaches. 2) Seek $10 MM Looking To Be A Billionaire. We Go Where $ Are. U Control $-We Trade Them	Current version July 12, 2019, 5.49 PM	Approved	US Hire Financial Guru	Approved

Money Debacle Soon-Pick Us #1 | BlackBox
+124% 2019; Model
[Ad] jackassbanker.com/Mr_Kelly_Trader/Extraordinaire

Trade & C Our Black Box In Action NYC Aug 9 & 10 $7500
Attendees Limited-Mr. Kelly Teaches. 2) Seek $10 MM
Looking To Be A Billionaire. We Go Where $ Are. U Control
$-We Trade Them.

Hedge Funds Losing Money?

Wanna Build A Hedge Fund?

📞 Call (917) 553-0030

Demacrash!

The second advertisement started running May 28, 2019 at 8:34am. It was also seen around the world using Google Ads.

The high for May 28th was 25,717.63. Remarkably, a 1,000 point drop kicked off two days later when President Trump announced a tariff on Mexican goods. The low on June 3, 2019 was 24,680.57.

Donald J. Trump ✔ @realDonaldTrump · May 30, 2019

On June 10th, the United States will impose a 5% Tariff on all goods coming into our Country from Mexico, until such time as illegal migrants coming through Mexico, and into our Country, STOP. The Tariff will gradually increase until the Illegal Immigration problem is remedied,...

Donald J. Trump ✔
@realDonaldTrump

....at which time the Tariffs will be removed. Details from the White House to follow.

♡ 99K   7:30 PM - May 30, 2019

💬 29.1K people are talking about this

Demacrash!

The third advertisement follows:

Version history ✕

GET READY FOR HISTORY'S WILDEST ROLLER COASTER RIDE

If President Trump implements the changes recommended in Chapter 3 of this book, the Dow *could exceed* the 40,000-50,000 range provided in the Dow forecast. It could even hit a peak of 55,000, or more, in a blow-off high. The "blow-off" high is the equivalent of the Dow Jones Industrial Average compared to August 1929 (adjusted using the author's proprietary inflation data). This was the peak of euphoria in buying stocks and the "high" just before the Great Depression. The staggering stock market crash came in October of the fall of that fateful year, 1929.

WHAT & WHEN TO BUY OCTOBER-DECEMBER, 2019

First of all, expect a "mini-Demacrash!" with a possible low on October 25 (+-/4 trading days), 2019. Weakness could easily run into January 2020. To technicians, this may look like a "spike-low" then a weak rally for a couple of weeks, then a retest or even break of that low to suck everybody into thinking the bull market was dead.

If there is a crash-like scenario in 2019's fall season, then this "crash" is expected to be relatively unspectacular in historic and in percentage terms. The Demacrash! forecast expects a 15-25% drop from approximately 27,000 (and change) on the Dow, down to the levels noted in the chart "Dow Jones Industrial Average 1998-2032 Trump Victory Forecast" as follows (see wave "4."), and as it was shown earlier in the chapter in full page mode on page 95.

Dow Jones Industrial Average 1998-2032
Trump Victory Forecast

Debt Apocalypse! -7

50000.00
45000.00
40000.00
35000.00
30000.00
25000.00
20000.00
15000.00
10000.00
5000.00
0.00

Wave 5: If Dow breaks above 37,000-it's likely heading between 40,000 and 50,000! Time frame for rally to end will be late 2023 - May, 2024.

Sell all positions no later than December 31, 2023!

Wave 4: Democrats will use every trick in the book to crush markets in the fall of 2019 and into 2020. Trump & team effectively fights back. A veritable battle of the ages is about to unfold.

All Dow/S&P long entries should be purchased in December 2019. If Trump weakly implements stimulus vis-a-vis this book's recommendations, a collapse could happen into the elections (i.e. November 2020).

27,719 ?
Fake-Out High?
27,398.68
DJIA High
July 16, 2019

2024 STOCK MARKET COLLAPSE LIKELY!
Lasts 6-8 years
Target low below 10,000 in 2032!

Gold & Commodity stocks are treated differently than regular equities.

The Democrats, if they lose in 2020, will leave no stone left unturned to crash the markets prior to 2024 elections. A Democrat victory in either 2020, or 2024, assures a crash scenario.

The forecast in this chart assumes a Trump VICTORY in 2024. If he loses—the big "CRASH" forecast to begin in 2024 will arrive early—catalyzed by the 2020 election defeat of Trump, and the socialist agenda of the Democrats being implemented during the last half of the 2020s!

Wave 4: Fast, Sharp, Scary Drop in Fall of 2019! This correction will look like the Bull Market is over! **Don't be fooled!!** The greatest rally of a lifetime is coming!! Target low for a late fall 2019 drop is 20,000 to 23,300. If the Dow hits 22,500, execute the buy on Dow & related stocks in this book. The coming "up" cycle will be huge-one of the biggest price moves ever seen.

9,900 ?
Multi-Year Low

© 2019 Robert L. Kelly
www.jackassbanker.com

If the Dow doesn't hit 22,500—buy equity DJIA/Big Cap positions when Dow rises over 28,000!

DEMACRASH! >>

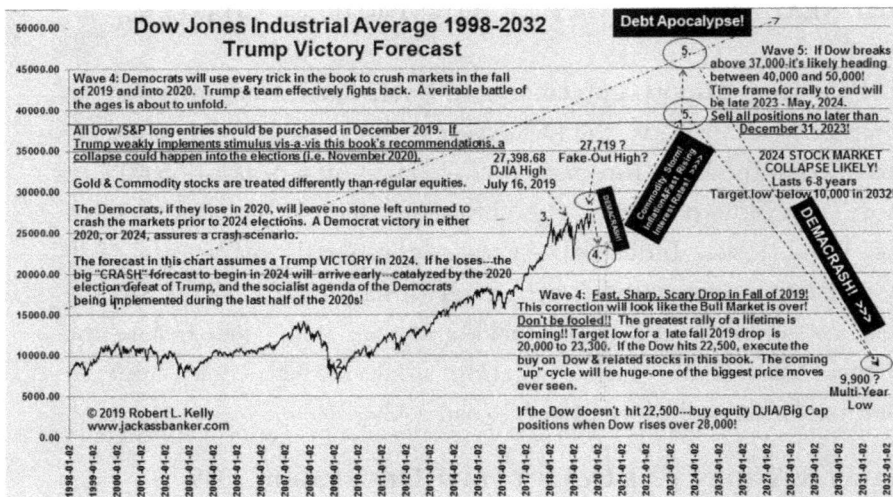

Important Note: If the forecast is incorrect for a correction into fall of 2019 (forecasting is a bit like trying to catch a falling knife.) and the market rallies through 28,000---then BUY. Upon seeing such strength of a breakout above 28,000 on the Dow, the risk will be NOT owning the market for the rocket-ride blast-off ahead.

After wave "4." down completes, you should expect a rip-roaring bull market to charge its way into most big-cap stocks---potentially right after October 25 (+-/4 days), but beginning no later than in late January of 2020. Bargain prices may be had in the fall of 2019. Again, however, if the underlying strength of this caged bull is great enough---it could just keep rallying. If it does, then pay attention to 28,000 on the Dow. A sustained break of this level to the upside means big cap stocks are taking off for the ride of a lifetime and you need to be on board.

Experienced investors are encouraged to pounce on any weakness during the fall of 2019 in various stocks on the "shopping list" of big cap securities printed in this book. Savvy investors know not all stocks (or other securities), bottom or top, at the same time.

The upside for big-cap stocks and certain other specialty sectors (as recommended in this book) is enormous. Being early in investing in this instance is far better than being late, because the rise in the markets will come, fast and furious---seemingly out of the blue.

If you buy early (e.g. between October and December 2019) and the market continues to correct into the election of November 2020---don't worry. The upside will swing your way, as clearly denoted in "Dow Jones Industrial Average 1998-2032 Trump Victory Forecast."

This means good targets for acquisition may be at hand if stocks go on sale in October 2019. Readers should place a heavy emphasis on blue chip stocks in the Dow Jones Industrial Average and S&P 500, along with the stocks recommended in the agricultural markets. This rally will be most robust with the big stocks---because that is where the liquidity will lie for the big money.

The markets have never seen anything like the panic buying which will occur in blue-chip stocks over the next few years. Buy on weakness.

Food Shortages

Food shortages caused by global *cooling* will cause nations to be scrambling to eat in the 2020s. This book does not address the fraud of global warming, which is a tax scheme to increase revenues for the out-of-money and broke Western governments. "Scientists" who support this environmental fraud are paid handsomely by governments to continue with this charade. Little do they realize, many people could actually die because there may not be enough food due to shortages brought on by cold temperatures and heated, but very short growing seasons---all brought on by our sun---not by human beings.

Demacrash!

What we are experiencing is global cooling likely caused by the solar minimum cycle. The "solar minimum" refers to sunspots---there aren't any on the sun in 2019.

Historically, when this lack of sun activity has been observed, there has been an increase in volcanic eruptions, worldwide. Too much ash in the air has caused crop failures for millennia, because ash blocks the sun and causes early winters and global cooling. However, one cannot "prove" this is precisely what is happening with sun spots. It is only an educated theory at this point. But, it makes a whole lot more sense than the zealots on television proclaiming we are all going to die of global warming in 12 years.

Chapter 5 lists various agricultural stocks to own until the end of 2023. The market may rally into May 2024, but the author's advice is to get out early. At that time, readers should sell everything in preparation for the huge Demacrash! expected to arrive in 2024. The markets themselves may even push to highs in May of 2024. It will then likely witness a debt collapse of galactic proportions---i.e. the "D'Apocalypse." This "Debt Apocalypse" takes place because of decades of horrible government spending policies, enormous deficits and rising interest rates---creating a derivatives debt and transaction collapse of the system.

This collapse will cause serious monetary issues and panic, with a total monetary reset via a new currency form, in all probability. Unprepared people will see anything they have sitting in banks, brokerage firms or other similar entities be the subject of seizure and rip off.

Whoever is in power will be desperate---and the money-printing will go wild, initially. This may actually cause stocks to march higher when interest rates rise dramatically---and then plunge as the economy turns down and government creates a new currency designed to steal money from depositors and investors via an unfavorable exchange rate. Confidence will collapse.

The world has seen this kind of action occur recently in Venezuela, where common stocks kept their value in relative terms by trending much higher---even when interest rates for the Bolivar, Venezuela's currency, soared. The reader can see the tremendous move up--- and then a tremendous crash of the "IBC," Venezuela's chief index, as political realities changed in the fall of 2018.

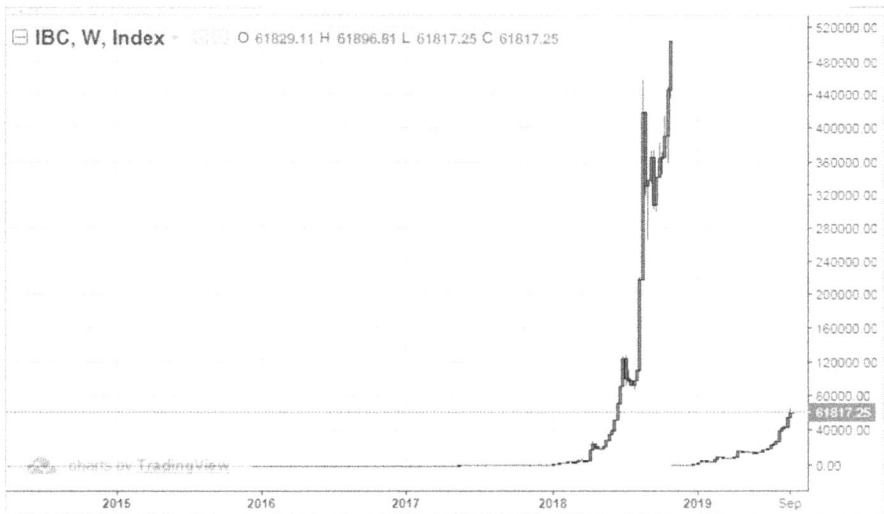

Source: (https://tradingeconomics.com/venezuela/stock-market, chart by TradingView.com).

The U.S. markets may produce a similar chart in the next several years. Trading and investing will be quite treacherous for the unprepared. High interest rates and international demand for U.S. currency (to pay U.S. Dollar denominated debt) cause a very strong dollar. The unexpected, relentless strength of the currency will be a major factor which causes the U.S. economy to grind to a halt.

When the market recognizes the game of musical chairs is about over, look out below. The invisible hand of Adam Smith will be at work. Because of the monetary abuse and outright monetization of every stock and bond problem in the markets over the course of nearly forty years, expect an economic crash, and a bad one, potentially the worst in history.

The following table provides you with Dow/Big Cap Stocks to own and tells you when to purchase them. Timing is important. For traders and aggressive investors, if you see the market crashing into the end of October 2019---and even into November, you should be purchasing any stocks crashing at that time on the list. Many of them may be at bargain prices. Suggested allocation for Dow/Big Cap stocks is 10% of a portfolio.

Dow/Big Cap Stocks-10%					
Date to Purchase Defense Stocks Below: Between October 25, 2019 - December 31, 2019					
Symbol	Name	Price 9/16/19	Yield	$ Market Cap	Comment
Dow/Big Cap Stocks:					
NFLX	Netflix	293.08		128.32 Billion	As trouble sets in across
FB	Facebook	186.17		523 Billion	Europe & Asia, and bond
MMM	MMM	168.89	3.41%	97.16 Billion	markets not yielding much
KO	Coca-Cola	53.8	2.97%	231.33 Billion	at the governmental level,
JNJ	Johnson & Johnson	129.92	2.92%	342.8 Billion	investors will turn to trusted
PFE	Pfizer	36.82	3.91%	203.6 Billion	names of stocks to buy. This
DD	Dupont	72.45	1.66%	54.01 Billion	means the need for liquidity.
VZ	Verizon	59.64	4.12%	246.67 Billion	
T	AT&T	37.28	5.47%	272.37 Billion	Big Cap stocks will be among
MSFT	Microsoft	136.32	1.35%	1.04 Trillion	the most liquid. This is only
UTX	United Technologies	137.7	2.14%	118.82 Billion	a partial list, but have been
MRK	Merck	82.1	2.66%	210.2 Billion	selected from leading names.
DIS	Disney	135.28	1.30%	244.5 Billion	Most bear decent dividend
CAT	Caterpillar	132.76	3%	74.68 Billion	yields.

The author is providing you a blue print for purchasing recommendations in this book---please, please remember: timing is *everything*.

While the author is bullish on Dow/Big Cap stocks, the author's *favorite* stocks are not on the Dow/Big Cap Stock list. The author adamantly believes **commodities** are going to shoot the moon in the next few years. He especially loves agriculturally-related stocks, as well as gold and silver miners---along with the shiny metals themselves.

A big word of caution: Over the next few years, free-market interest rates will be dramatically increasing. This presents a risk factor for any highly-leveraged companies---including Disney, for example, especially after purchasing Fox. Disney's success will ultimately rely on having enough profits to cover debt amortization and experiencing a successful adaptation of their streaming technology, worldwide (or perhaps finding themselves the target of a takeover). From a technological perspective, Netflix has a huge lead in streaming and it is a better bet in that department. Both stocks will likely rise in the run up, however.

If you are not concerned with dividends, and do not want to stock pick---buy the "Diamonds"---symbol "DIA." It tracks the Dow.

The rush into U.S. equities will be driven by FOMO (i.e. the Fear of Missing Out) and the uncertainty of *where* to invest major capital on behalf of sovereign states, along with pension and hedge funds. The demand for U.S. assets will be high among international citizens investing in U.S. big-cap stocks and bonds. They, along with the big money managers, will set off a scramble for big, liquid stocks of successful companies, with everyone driven by FOMO.

This will be a race by money managers worldwide, to park money to ensure liquidity. This means, first and foremost, investing in the U.S. markets. Stocks with a decent dividend yield are a plus, even in an increasing interest-rate environment.

Today, the bond market is at all-time bubble highs in long, medium and short-term bonds. Expect chaos to erupt in the bond market and DO NOT, UNDER ANY CIRCUMSTANCES invest in any security which keeps hold of your money for more than one year--- even if you have to pay short term to have access to cash. Do not listen to the fear-mongers telling you rates in the United States are going to "zero." If they do, it will be for a very short period of time (likely the fall of 2019 and into 2020).

Long term bonds are going to get crushed. They will lose pension funds and long-term bond investors hundreds of billions of dollars beginning in 2020, if not sooner.

Defense stocks are a good hedge to have in a portfolio into the 2020's because of the threat of war. Even a localized/regionalized conflict will cause these stocks to rise. As of the printing of this book they are a bit expensive, but if there is a fall sell-off, there may be bargains to be had. Only a small allocation (e.g. 5%) is suggested for this group.

Defense Stocks-Investment Allocation 5%
Date to Purchase Defense Stocks Below: Between October 25, 2019 - December 31, 2019

Symbol	Name	Price 9/16/19	Yield	$ Market Cap	Comment
Defense Stocks:					
TDG	Transdigm Group	521.67	0%	27.84 Billion	Component maker drones
LMT	Lockheed Martin	392.23	2.24%	1110.76 Billion	Aircraft
NOC	Northrup Grumman	370.08	1.43%	62.62 Billion	Aircraft
BA	Boeing	378.81	2.17%	213.16 Billion	Planes, aerospace, defense
HII	Huntington Ingalls Industries	226.66	1.54%	9.2 Billion	Ship building, cybersecurity
GD	General Dynamics	189.97	2.15%	54.87 Billion	Ships & submarines
RTN	Raytheon	204.16	1.85%	56.86 Billion	Missile defense
LDOS	Leidos Holdings, Inc.	86.16	1.58%	12.39 Billion	Defense contractor
HXL	Hexcel	82.62	82.00%	7.03 Billion	Carbon Fiber Materials
KTOS	Kratos	21.64	0%	2.3 Billion	Drones, laser weapons

The next group of highly liquid stocks of interest is "big oil." Definitely, do not purchase these stocks until after October 25, 2019 and preferably in January 2020, late in the month, unless they crash in October-November-December.

Major Oil Stocks-Investment Allocation 5%

Symbol	Name	Price 9/1619	Yield	Date to Purchase
CVX	Chevron Corporation	124	3.40%	This list of stocks may be
PSX	Phillips	103.49	3.48%	purchased between October
VLO	Valero Energy	81.47	44.20%	25, 2019 and December 1,
XOM	Exxon	73.93	4.71%	2019. If the market is
HES	Hess Corporation	69.32	1.44%	crashing at the end of
COP	ConocoPhillips	61.38	1.99%	October 2019, some real
TOT	Total SA	52.95	6.88%	bargains may be available.
OXY	Occidental Petroleum	48.1	6.57%	Purchasing during a crash
BP	British Petroleum plc	39.18	6.28%	should only be attempted
MRO	Marathon Oil Corporation	13.96	1.43%	by advanced investors.

Oil stocks may be due for a major drop, which should create outstanding yields on many of them, especially the largest companies. Not all sectors bottom at the same time, and with a global slowdown hitting the market, oil prices could get hit hard in the fall/winter of 2019-2020.

Watch for a "crash" as any kind of big price drop into the end of October/Year End 2019 could spell bargains in the oil sector, with big moves down of 20-40% possibly.

REMEMBER---SELL ALL STOCKS, EVERYTHING, NO LATER THAN DECEMBER 2023 EVEN THOUGH A RALLY IS EXPECTED INTO MAY 2024. IT WILL BE BETTER TO GET OUT EARLY FROM THIS ROCKET RIDE, THAN OUT TOO LATE!

THE LONGER YOU HOLD ANY SECURITIES, THE GREATER THE SYSTEMIC RISK. ANYTHING CAN HAPPEN AT ANY TIME TO CAUSE A DERIVATIVES COLLAPSE IN THE YEARS AHEAD.

FOR THE MOST CONSERVATIVE INVESTORS, GOING TO CASH IN A PRIVATE VAULT WITH PRECIOUS METALS AND ASSETS OF TANGIBLE VALUE MAY BE VERY WISE STARTING AT THE END OF DECEMBER 2023.

THIS SIGNIFICANT RECOMMENDATION IS IN ANTICIPATION OF A GLOBAL SHIFT TO A SINGLE CURRENCY, BROUGHT ON BY A DRAMATIC CREDIT CRISIS. THE RESULT WILL BE THE THEFT OF THOUSANDS OF BILLIONS (i.e. TRILLIONS) OF DOLLARS BY THE BANKS AND GOVERNMENTS THROUGH AN EXCHANGE RATE FORMULA WHICH LEAVES HISTORICAL DOLLAR, EURO, YEN, POUND AND EVEN YUAN HOLDERS "HOLDING THE BAG." DON'T GET CAUGHT IN THEIR TRAP.

ANY STOCKS OR BONDS YOU INSIST ON OWNING MAKE SURE YOU HAVE THE ORIGINAL CERTIFICATES OF OWNERSHIP (IF POSSIBLE).

THE COMING DEBT AND DERIVATIVES CRISIS WILL TAKE DOWN GIANTS OF INDUSTRY AND THE U.S. CONGRESS AND BRUSSELS' BUREAUCRATS HAVE RIGGED THE SYSTEM WITH THE BANKS AND BROKERS TO MAKE IT LEGAL TO STEAL YOUR ASSETS IF THEY ARE IN THEIR POSSESSION.

THIS INCLUDES CASH IN THE BANK, STOCKS, BONDS AND ANYTHING IN A BANK-HELD SAFE-DEPOSIT BOX AND THE ETFs WHICH PURPORTEDLY "HOLD" GOLD AND SILVER (OR OTHER ASSETS). IF THEY CLEAR THEIR TRADES THROUGH A BROKERAGE FIRM OR AN EXCHANGE (WHICH THEY ALL DO), YOU MAY NEVER SEE ANY OF THE ASSETS YOU BELIEVED WERE PLEDGED AS COLLATERAL. 2024 TO THE 2030's WILL BE FRAUGHT WITH DIFFICULTY.

FINALLY, AND MOST IMPORTANTLY: CONSULT YOUR FINANCIAL ADVISER BEFORE MAKING ANY INVESTMENT DECISIONS.

WARNING...WARNING...WARNING...WARNING
PLEASE REREAD THE ABOVE EIGHT PARAGRAPHS!

CHAPTER 5

COMMODITY MARKET FORECAST

How can you say BULLISH in every language on earth?

Yes, that's right: **SNORT**!!! If you listen, there is a bull clawing his hoofs to run out of the gate and his horns are very sharp.

It is a big bull, too. Its pent-up energy is readying to bust out, sky-high in the agricultural sector, particularly with respect to actual commodity prices. This forlorn group has been abandoned by nearly everyone. This makes the perfect ingredient for relatively low-risk, high-reward investing. Stocks in this sector are also fairly liquid, and may be vehicles for investors seeking growth with liquidity.

It is no secret this author believes global warming is a big hoax which was brought on by out-of-money governments to tax big oil and consumers of fossil fuels. What the nincompoops in bureaucracy do not understand, because they have not read history, is the fact weather is a cyclical phenomenon driven largely by our Sun.

Careful reading of the "science" purportedly behind global warming from NASA, NOAA, the Europeans, etc. shows rampant manipulation of data---favoring a global warming verdict.

This is a completely false narrative, and not particularly shocking given the spin we hear on news every night on television these days.

At times, the misleading broadcasts make it seem like propaganda is being foisted on the viewers by all media channels---just like the Nazis and Communists did when they overthrew their existing governments to seize power. After a while, of course, the people revolted. Some sooner than others...

As discussed, the truth is what people should be preparing for is **COLD**, caused by the solar minimum cycle (see page 104). The cold has nothing to do with "climate change" due to man. It has everything to do with the solar minimum.

Regardless, this book is not intended to launch a debate about the environment. The reader may take the advice of the author, or not. In fact, the reader may still believe in global warming and still take advantage of the many stock opportunities in the agriculture sector (as well as other recommendations in this book). Free choice is a great right in the United States.

COMING CROP FAILURES

Under a scenario, however, where governments and grant recipients are creating fake global warming research (which is really conspiratorially manipulated weather data to justify carbon taxes on industry and individuals), and what is really coming at us is extreme cold, then we should expect to see *early frosts* and *crop failures* in the years ahead.

If the author was super aggressive, he would invest 75% of funds in the agricultural sector and eliminate big oil and claw back from other groups to compose a 100% investment allocation. His favorite aggressive agricultural ETFs are listed first. They are from the Teucrium Fund family, and are designed to track the price of corn, wheat and soybeans with futures and other derivative products. This makes them highly volatile, so invest accordingly. In a major bull market in this sector, these three ETFs may be among the top performers.

For more conservative investors, the author provides the reader with a lengthy list of agriculture-industry stocks, most of which even bear a decent dividend yield.

In this list beware of "Bayer." They own Monsanto, except for certain seed and pesticide businesses which were sold off when they acquired the company. Bayer's yield looks enticing, but this company faces serious litigation from cancer-causing chemicals (e.g. "Roundup") created by Monsanto.

Agricultural Stocks-Investment Allocation 50%
Date to Purchase Agricultural Indexes and the Stocks Below: Immediately and <u>Before December 31, 2019</u>

Symbol	Name	Price 9/16/19	Yield	$ Market Cap/Comment	Date to Purchase

Note: ETFs & Stocks on this list should outperform many other stocks. Shortages of food in the years ahead will cause consumers to see dramatic increases in food prices, as a result. This will translate into record earnings for food companies and a PANIC to buy them. It is important to BUY THEM NOW OR ASAP! Diversification is important.

Symbol	Name	Price 9/16/19	Yield	$ Market Cap/Comment	Note:
Agricultural ETFs:					Note:
CORN	Teucrium Corn Fund	14.92		88.06 Million Net Assets	ETFs & stocks on this list
WEAT	Teucrium Wheat	5.25		46.99 Million Net Assets	should outperform the "Dow."
SOYB	Teucrium Soybean	15.45		27.73 Million Net Assets	Agriculture will see extreme
					shortages of food & dramatic
Agricultural stocks:					increases in food prices!
DE	Deere	164.5	1.86%	51.8 Billion	Tractors & Equipment
SAFM	Sanderson Farms	154.08	0.83%	3.41 Billion	Poultry
SMG	Scotts Miracle-Gro Company	101.20	2.29%	5.62 Billion	Seeds, fertilizers, chemicals
CVGW	Calavo Growers	93.88	1.70%	$1.65 Billion	Vegetables
TSN	Tyson Foods	85.94	1.75%	25.32 Billion	Beef, pork, poultry
FMC	FMC Corp	90.67	1.76%	11.83 Billion	Diversified
CMP	Compass Minerals Intl	57.37	5.02%	1.94 Billion	Salt & chemicals
NTR	Nutrien	51.61	3.33%	29.67 Billion	Fertilizer-Owns Monsanto
CF	CF Industries	50.51	2.38%	11.03 Billion	Fertilizer
CALM	Cal-Maine Foods	45.34	1.89%	2.21 Billion	Eggs
ADM	Archer Daniels Midland	41.66	3.36%	23.2 Billion	Ethanol, feed, supplements
CTVA	Corteva	29.10	1.79%	21.75 Billion	Chemicals, Fertilizer & Seeds
PPM	Pilgrim's Pride	30.86	0%	7.69 Billion	Poultry
FDM	Fresh Del Monte Produce	31.87	0.75%	1.54 Billion	Fruits & Vegetables
BAYRY	Bayer	18.7	8.53%	17.44 Billion	Seeds, agricultural chemicals
CZZ	Cosan	15.26	0.54%	3.64 Billion	Sugar, ethanol, fuel
GPRE	Green Plains	10.72	4.48%	409.16	Ethanol, feed, grains
DF	Dean Foods	1.44	8.30%	132.79 Million	Dairy products

Likewise with Dean Foods; they are a big dairy player, but beware of problems. Hundreds of milk alternatives have invaded the marketplace and the company has debt issues. Margins at the dairy level have been getting smashed. It is vital to this industry's and company's business that the dairy industry recovers, fast.

If these companies (e.g. Bayer without filing bankruptcy and Dean Foods living through its economic nightmare) survive, they should see prices stage impressive recoveries in their respective stocks. In each case be careful. Either could easily file a "Chapter 11" bankruptcy if debts or liabilities become too big to handle. That action would negatively impact their common stock prices. The author would consider these highly speculative positions at this point---until all the issues are brought to light.

Looking past these two potential crap shoots, many of the great companies in the U.S. and international food chains are listed in the preceding "Agricultural Stocks" table. An investment allocation of 50% is recommended. These stocks should be purchased *immediately* as they are all suffering from the continued trade conflict with China. The bad news on China trade is highly likely to have already been priced into their common stocks.

Any additional temporary drop into October-December 2019 should be treated as a gift. There is no assurance this will happen.

At this point, once again, the risk is **NOT** owning this sector aggressively.

China will be in for a big surprise when they can't feed their people during the 2020s.

SNORT!!!

CHAPTER 6

PRECIOUS METALS MARKET FORECAST

The precious metals will be a bit tricky in the fall of 2019. They have had a great rally, and in the Jackass Banker trading demonstrations carried out in 2019, the Black Box was steadfastly bullish on the shiny metals. Long term, the outlook is extremely bullish, meaning specifically, the price of gold may even hit $5,000/ounce in the next several years. Published February 19, 2014 in <u>D'Apocalypse Now!</u> the author provided this chart for gold's overall roadmap:

FEBRUARY 2014 PUBLISHED GOLD FORECAST

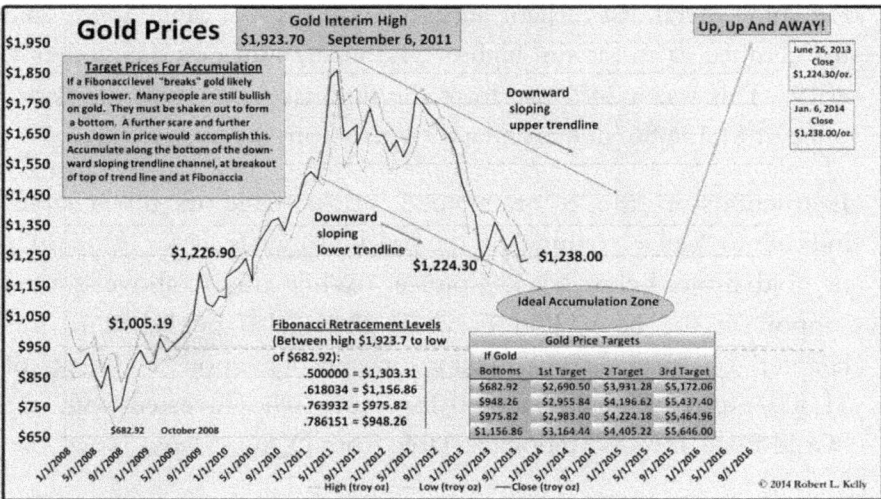

The original "Gold Price Targets" in this chart are still valid---that is, if you are lucky enough to have gold drop down in price, again. Here are the bottom targets and projected upside prices.

Gold Price Targets			
If Gold Bottoms	**1st Target**	**2 Target**	**3rd Target**
$682.92	$2,690.50	$3,931.28	$5,172.06
$948.26	$2,955.84	$4,196.62	$5,437.40
$975.82	$2,983.40	$4,224.18	$5,464.96
$1,156.86	$3,164.44	$4,405.22	$5,646.00

Those who followed the "Accumulation Zone" target oval on the previous chart, and the "Gold Price Targets" Fibonacci accumulation table above, have done extremely well for themselves.

The first possible bottom predicted ($1,156.86/ounce) it turns out, provided readers with pinpoint instructions as to what price to "buy" gold. The subsequent low on November 26, 2015 (21 months after publication of this gold chart and table) of $1,069.20/ounce gave ample opportunity for readers to purchase the shiny metal at excellent accumulation prices. Since then, gold has climbed to an interim high of $1,556.20/ounce on September 4, 2019. This was a 34% rise from the Fibonacci accumulation target price of $1,156.86/ounce and a 45% rise from the low, so far.

Instructions in the recommended stocks table in this chapter indicate to "sell everything" in the precious metals sector if the price of gold drops below $1,300/ounce. While this is above quoted support in the new Gold Forecast chart (also published in this chapter on page 120), locking in profits upon a break of $1,300/ounce is sound advice for those who invested with the "Gold Price Targets" Fibonacci table from D'Apocalypse Now!

Investors should let the market do its work and see if support, noted at $1,230-$1,280 on the Gold Forecast chart, holds. If supports breaks, the odds are high gold will test some of the Fibonacci "If Gold Bottoms" levels noted in the "Gold Price Targets" table. With a breakdown (especially below the low of $1,069.20/ounce), be on the lookout for a once-in-a-lifetime opportunity to "load the truck up" and buy as much gold and silver as you can below $1,000/ounce.

Specific targets are listed but, don't get greedy when the underlying targets are $975.82, $948.26 and $682.92. If the price of gold drops below $1,000 (which this author does not think is the most probable outcome) just BUY. Precious metals are notorious for SPIKING in scary upward and downward "spikes" and if the metal is dropping into a spike…don't be afraid. **BUY MORE.**

The upside for gold and silver given the economic apocalypse of a debt contagion, is enormous. Some readers who bought gold on the first drop to $1,069.20, with the target entry price published at $1,156.86, already have nice profits. In 2013, when the author was writing D'Apocalypse Now! and created his gold forecast, gold was trading nearly $1,500/ounce. Purchasing the metal using the accumulation table as a guide at the first Fibonacci retracement bottoming price, investors are now sitting on 39% profits at the interim high made in September 2019.

To lock in profits (but, to repurchase gold later again as it gets cheaper), these investors may want to take profits upon a drop to $1300. Then…wait for support and see if the price of gold breaks down (see Gold Forecast chart). If it does, then follow the accumulation target "If Gold Bottoms" prices to repurchase the shiny metals, once again.

For most people, the above instructions are a little too detailed, because the message for the shiny metals is nothing but bullish going out into the middle 2020s. If you are not a trader, you should just hold on to your holdings and wait for the big move up.

Demacrash!

The first true launch of the metals upward will likely be extremely violent. Most people will be afraid to buy once the enormous price rise begins, because the metals may have *just* experienced a big spike **down.** This is usually the fake-out move by very big money before prices soar. Look for this kind of move down in fall 2019.

For gold and silver, enormous spikes "up" frequently occur upon the advent of a major black swan incident (e.g. war, a sovereign debt crisis, bank closures and/or general panic). It is also for this reason long term investors *should just hold on to what they own* and do not play it "cute" with the detailed trading instructions in this chapter.

You might have to ride out a bit of a correction (yes, even a scary one below $1,000/ounce), but patience will reward you as you won't be left without any gold or silver if the balloon goes up, and you wake up overnight and---BOOM! Gold is trading like Bitcoin.

The Author cannot emphasize this risk enough: **the risk in gold is not owning it.** You may go to bed one evening and wake up with the price of gold doubling overnight (silver, also).

If one looks at the equity chart and the gold chart, it is easy to see the author's thinking.

Basically, if Trump "wins" the standoff with the Democrats in the financial markets (i.e. the Democrats fail to create a "Demacrash!" into the fall elections of November 2020), gold has a good chance of seeing a correction---and a good sized one below $1,000/ounce.

However, if the Democrats "win" and pull all their aces out, successfully cut a deal with the Fed and the banks to create a new currency, monetary system, or such other critical change to the monetary system favorable to the banks, then gold will soar.

Fear is the contagion which will drive gold to $5,000/ounce and that fear, whatever drives it, will run through the Fed's veins, as well. This will likely cause a flood of money printing and quantitative easing which will dwarf the $30 Trillion Heist.

Hello, $5,000/ounce!

President Trump always says he likes to win. This author is betting on the President to win the election in 2020 and fight off attacks on the market (and himself) by Democrats and their allies. They all hate him so much they would rather ruin markets than see him get re-elected.

If the President is successful, it is certainly a possibility to see a correction in gold, but in major bull markets, those corrections can be very minor and brief. **This is why the author is providing instructions to make sure you own precious metals no later than December 1, 2019, unless you see a breakdown below $1069.20.** Then make your gold purchases in accordance with the Fibonacci table provided in this chapter.

If after a breakdown of $1069.20 the price of gold rises back above $1,400/ounce you should BUY gold to a maximum allocation, immediately. Such price action may indicate the shiny metal is likely going to blast through the roof.

Interestingly, this is where gold is today, above $1,400/ounce and trying to decide if it is going to blastoff NOW….or LATER.

Again, the next year of possible price gyrations in gold will be irrelevant for long-term investors in the shiny metals.

The metals will soar in the 2020s. The new Gold Forecast chart follows:

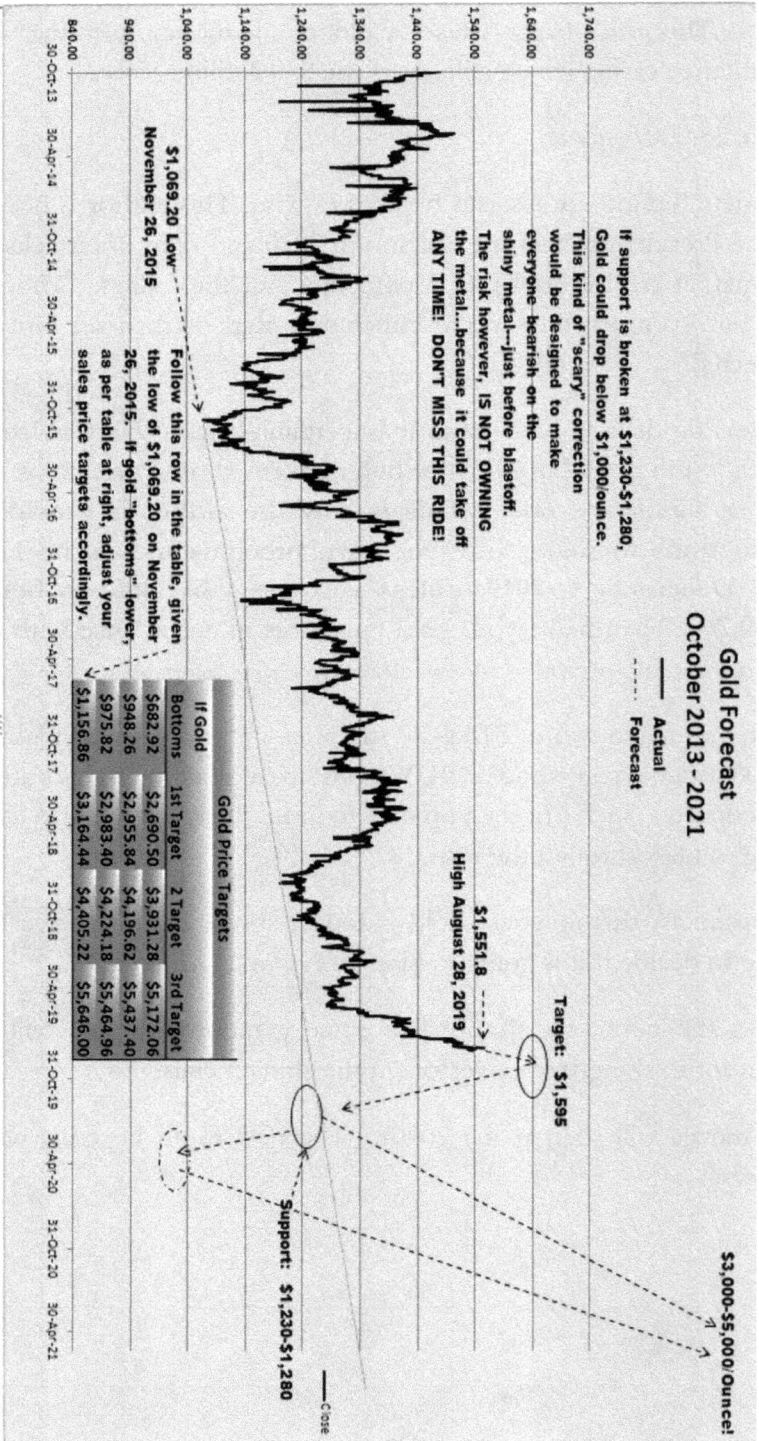

Gold Forecast
October 2013 - 2021

—— Actual
----- Forecast

If support is broken at $1,230-$1,280, Gold could drop below $1,000/ounce. This kind of "scary" correction would be designed to make everyone bearish on the shiny metal—just before blastoff. The risk however, IS NOT OWNING the metal...because it could take off ANY TIME! DON'T MISS THIS RIDE!

$1,551.8 ----->
High August 28, 2019

Target: $1,595

Support: $1,230-$1,280

$3,000-$5,000/Ounce!

$1,069.20 Low
November 26, 2015

Follow this row in the table, given the low of $1,069.20 on November 26, 2015. If gold "bottoms" lower, as per table at right, adjust your sales price targets accordingly.

Gold Price Targets			
If Gold			
Bottoms	1st Target	2 Target	3rd Target
$682.92	$2,690.50	$3,931.28	$5,172.06
$948.26	$2,955.84	$4,196.62	$5,437.40
$975.87	$2,983.40	$4,224.18	$5,464.96
$1,156.86	$3,164.44	$4,405.22	$5,646.00

—— Close

30-Oct-13 30-Apr-14 31-Oct-14 30-Apr-15 31-Oct-15 30-Apr-16 31-Oct-16 30-Apr-17 31-Oct-17 30-Apr-18 31-Oct-18 30-Apr-19 31-Oct-19 30-Apr-20 31-Oct-20 30-Apr-21

840.00 940.00 1,040.00 1,140.00 1,240.00 1,340.00 1,440.00 1,540.00 1,640.00 1,740.00

120

PRECIOUS METALS STOCK SELECTION

A stock table of recommended precious metals securities follows. This list is presented to allow you to build a portfolio. Since everyone's availability of capital is different, these publicly traded securities provide a range of choices. Some are aggressive, while others represent fairly large, established mining operations, a bit more "conservative" in this highly volatile sector.

Before making any investments, readers should investigate and verify the information in all tables and charts presented in this book. While the author works hard to try and ensure information is indeed correct, many times what is printed (or taken directly from annual reports) is incorrect and, of course, calculations, uploading data, and typing are prone to error.

Nevertheless, the securities listed in the "Precious Metals" table present interesting opportunities. In precious metals bull markets, mining stocks particularly, can outperform the metals themselves.

Pay attention to the "Current Ratio" listed in this table for each company. The higher it is the better. Current Ratio is a measure of current assets to current liabilities of a company. Also important are the Debt/Equity ratios. The lower the better; this represents the amount of debt a company has, divided by its equity.

Mining operations are capital intensive and because of an increasing interest rate environment in the early 2020's especially, many mining companies may declare bankruptcy because of debt. In this list, the author has tried to screen for low debt. It is hoped this will provide some peace of mind to the investor.

Make sure you do your own due diligence, and consult with your financial adviser before purchasing anything. There are thousands of mining stocks, ETFs and funds out there and this list merely represents a few of them, relatively speaking.

Obviously, some of the low-priced stocks carry very high risk. Invest especially carefully with those stocks and read financial statements of any company before making an investment. Things can change quickly with smaller mining companies, particularly. Make sure you spread out your investments and diversify. The entire precious metals sector is highly risky.

Each security in the table has its name and stock symbol listed. Various indexes, funds and ETFs which may be interesting for a bull market in metals are also listed, along with the futures symbols for both gold and silver.

Most of the table is composed of companies which maintain or operate, mining operations in the precious metals sector.

This sector is weighted less than the agricultural sector for the reason "Ag" stocks have been beaten up and are ready to go on a tear upwards. They also do not have as much hype surrounding them as the metals, either.

Gold bugs basically ruin the precious metals market for regular investors because they are always preaching "BUY, BUY, BUY!"--- just like Randolph and Mortimer Duke did when Eddie Murphy and Dan Aykroyd put them in the poor house in the famous movie, "Trading Places." Poor Randolph and Mortimer---buying and selling at the wrong time put them on skid row.

Gold bugs seem to buy no matter what the price, even just before the price collapses. Remember: gold is just a trade, it is not a religion. The work of the author tries to take advantage of change in markets. No market goes straight up and the probabilities of making money rise with discipline. Stick to good companies, targeted investment levels and timeframes.

You may build yourself a "gold mine" of good fortune, as a result.

Precious Metals-Investment Allocation 30%

Date to Purchase Precious Metals Indexes, Stocks & the Metal itself: December 1, 2019

Timing is everything! Gold & Silver will likely consolidate in the fall of 2019. Make sure you own them by December 1, 2019!

Symbol	Name	Price 9/16/19	Yield	$ Market Cap/Comment	Warning	Current Ratio	Debt/Equity
Precious Metal Indexes:							
GDX	Gold Miners Index	27.4	0.38%	22.05 Billion			
GDXJ	Junior Gold Miners Index	37.5	0.37%	22.03 Billion			
JNUG	Junior Gold Miners Index	64.81		JNUG is only for aggressive investors! 3X Performance.			
NUGT	3X Gold Performance	30.65		NUGT is only for aggressive investors! 3X Performance.			
SLVP	iShares Silver Miners	10.09		$82.45 Million			
GLD	ETF - Gold	141.76		40.74 Billion			
SLV	ETF - Silver	16.78		5.8 Billion			
Gold & Silver Futures:							
GC	Gold Futures	1511.3		For aggressive & sophisticated investors only.			
SI	Silver Futures	18.01		For aggressive & sophisticated investors only.			
Precious Metals Stocks:							
MAG	MAG Silver Corp	11.30		.976 Billion	A diversified mining portfolio provides balance. Gold & silver miners with low Debt/Equity rations tilt the odds in favor of success. Some miners could become bankrupt, as many borrow too much money. Also, if a miner hedges its production, it will likely limit its profit when gold breaks out. REMEMBER: Gold could STILL correct below $1000/ounce in 2020! If gold drops below $1300/ounce, close all precious metals positions. Reopen them when/if gold drops below $1,000/ounce—OR if gold rises above $1600/ounce. We expect gold to climb up to perhaps $5,000/ounce in the years ahead.	251.7	0.01
EXK	Endeavor Silver Corp.	2.45		336.82 Million		3.3	0.02
RGLD	Royal Gold	123.13	0.86%	8.07 Billion		4.6	0.1
PAAS	Pan American Silver	16.61	0.01%	3.48 Billion		4.1	0.15
EGO	El Dorado	8.37		1.33 Billion		2.2	0.16
GPL	Great Panther	0.73		231.25 Million		1	0.18
WPM	Wheaton Precious Metals	26.88	1.34%	11.98 Billion		3.6	0.22
HMY	Harmony Gold	3.08	2.10%	1.66 Billion		1.4	0.23
BVN	Buenaventura	14.73	1.02%	4.05 Billion		1.9	0.24
AGI	Alamos Gold	6.27	0.32%	2.73 Billion		2.9	0.25
SSRM	SSR Mining	14.42		1.76 Billion		4	0.27
FSM	Fortuna Silver	3.48		609.43 Million		3.57	0.33
HL	Hecla Mining	1.94	0.51%	953.54 Million		1.2	0.36
GOLD	Barrick	17.15		30.15 Billion		2.5	0.37
CDE	Couer Mining	4.76		1.06 Billion		1	0.41
AG	First Majestic	9.76		2.09 Billion		3.13	0.51
AU	AngloGold Ashanti	19.46	0.34%	8.21 Billion		0.9	0.82
NGD	New Gold	1.26		847.81 Million		2.1	0.91
Canadian Extremely High Risk---use very small asset allocation % to these:							
SB	Stratabound Minerals	0.055		2.09 Million		2.24	0.06
JAEG	Jaeger Resources	0.02		961.68 Thousand	JAEG has negative equity.	0.02	Infinite

If you haven't done anything in precious metals yet, the suggestion is to wait until no later than December 1, 2019. The fall months, before Christmas, often see lows in the precious metals. If there is a correction, it would be a good time to buy. Finally, if you "miss" the chance to purchase gold, then on a sustained breakout above $1,600, you should establish a position, knowing you are at risk on the downside. However, if the underlying cause of the rise is due to panic, or some kind of black swan event brewing, then your risk is *not* owning any gold. You might regret not owning gold when the shiny metal races above $2,000/ounce, perhaps on its way to $5,000.

$1,600/ounce is the "fail-safe" number, but the previous instructions to own gold and maximize your allocation still holds on a break-back above $1,400/ounce---if gold drops below $1,069.20.

GOLD'S RELATIVE VALUE IN DEFLATION

Finally, 2025+ may see dramatic deflation in large numbers of sectors. This will be caused by failed monetary systems due to massive overspending, persistent deficits, high interest rates, and unpaid debts which create a Molotov Cocktail igniting a global derivatives bonfire and collapse.

This will translate into failed states in the future because of their debt encumbrances in many overleveraged countries (e.g. Argentina, Italy, Spain, Portugal, etc.). It also means a collapsing EU. And it means there is real risk of a dramatic drop in the confidence of the United States Government.

This may begin seriously as soon as 2024.

With towering mountains of debt in nearly every country on earth, this cannot end well. Paper money may not even be worth the paper it is printed on and the real prices of goods, services and especially real estate, will drop like rocks in the ocean as people will not have any currency of value to barter with and the banks will refuse to lend to nearly everyone.

This may lead to the paradox of parabolically high prices in currency terms---and lower prices in gold terms---as government money presses go to work.

Real estate prices in most markets, are expected to **keep** falling through 2030, at least. Florida and Texas are possible exceptions, as they become tax havens. Real estate is simply one of the most illiquid assets anyone can own, especially if the banks stop lending and they start squeezing during a depression.

This is what the author predicts will occur, likely starting in 2024, but certainly in 2025+.

At that time, Gold prices may ultimately drop from their higher Fibonacci target levels (e.g. approximately $2,600-$5,600/ounce), however, the relative value of gold and numismatic gold coins particularly, will hold. There is an old saying that a one-ounce real-gold coin could buy one of the finest men's suits in 1900 and it still can today, if you purchase high-quality fabric and Hong Kong tailoring and not a fashion-oriented brand name.

CAUTION COUNTERFEIT COINS & BARS

Finally, if you invest in precious metal coins or bars, make sure you investigate and find a private vault to store your precious metals and other assets. Make certain any precious metals you have purchased have been checked for being potential counterfeits. This is no joke.

The Chinese and others can manufacture a laser-etched, near-perfect golden foil (copying any coin on earth) around tungsten, a near-worthless metal. Unless there is specialized machinery, or other tools known to the gold trade, the atomic difference in weights between gold and tungsten are only a couple of atoms of difference, and indistinguishable to humans (Tungsten = 183.84 u, atomic number 74, while Gold = 196.96657 u and carries atomic number 79).

Purchase your coins from a professional who uses XRF Spectrometry. Counterfeiters are even packaging counterfeit coins in nearly identical NGC (i.e. "Numismatic Grading Corporation") slabs. Slabs are a plastic cover over the coin with a bar code---making it impossible for an untrained eye to tell any difference at all between a true gold coin inside the slab and a counterfeit one.

There are many, many stories of counterfeit coins and bars published today, even at the central bank level. The Federal Reserve of New York purportedly sent an entire shipment of gold bars to Hong Kong, only to have it returned because there were fake bars populating within.

Do your research on *where* you are purchasing your gold and silver coins and/or bars. Because of the risk of making the ownership of gold illegal, also purchase gold for your "collection" and only purchase numismatic coins. This is important.

In Germany, Angela Merkel recently announced that any gold dealer must report their buyers to the state, supposedly to track money laundering and terrorists. This is just a lie, of course. The authorities want tax money and will do anything to get it

Numismatic coins have some historic or aesthetic value. For gold coins, go for older ones which are not "rare." Many of these have been trading hands for a long time. These coins are preferred and check them out to ensure they are not counterfeit. Counterfeit coins can be laser etched to look old, also.

Silver is in the same category. Purchasing bags of old silver coins from a reliable source for a collection would likely be safer than buying brand new American Silver Eagles. Silver is also susceptible to being counterfeited.

Know your source. Treachery is everywhere in the gold bar, gold coin, silver coin and silver bar markets.

CHAPTER 7

BOND MARKET FORECAST

Long-term corporate bond prices, especially junk bonds, will collapse. Emerging market debt will have leprosy. Rates will sky rocket and longer term bonds will get routed. This is about all you need to know in this sector: Do not, under any circumstances, invest in any bond from any source that is longer than one year in maturity.

Likewise for Certificates of Deposit, which this book does not recommend; CDs are dependent on the liquidity and viability of banks. FDIC and private insurance will not mean anything in a systemic failure brought on by rising interest rates. The sheer number of failures will dwarf the system. Everyone should remember the banking and money market scare of the credit crisis, insurance companies went broke overnight. The same will be true for D'Apocalypse, but much, much worse.

Without stating the obvious, never put your money into a "money-market" fund. The SEC revised regulations which now permit the manager of any fund to change the $1.00 unit price to anything it wants if liquidations occur en masse. The **only** money market fund worthwhile is a U.S. Government **short term** money market fund. But, you will need to get your money out of the brokerage firm before the debt collapse hits the system. It would be far, far better to purchase short-term U.S. Treasury Bills directly from: https://www.treasurydirect.gov/indiv/research/indepth/tbills/res_tbill_buy.htm.

What you will be looking at in the mid-to-late 2020s is a situation where there will be global confiscation of wealth, with assurances that your monies and/or assets will be converted into a new currency at a "fair" price.

As you might guess, this will be one big rip-off scheme to steal wealth, gobble up sovereign assets, takeover industry giants, and solidify the banks as the captains over the administration of a "one-world" global currency. This currency will likely be digital, with local currency administration by state/country.

Without wasting time, the following is a definitive list of the largest junk bond ETFs, as of September 4, 2019 in the United States. These will make tremendous short sales in the years ahead.

If you sell short (i.e. definitely do not own them) any of these, stick with the "top three" names on the list because they have the most liquidity. "HYG" and "JNK" will be most liquid in all probability, making it easier to borrow shares to sell these ETFs short.

	High Yield Bond ETFs				
	September 19, 2019				
Symbol	ETF Name	Total Assets*	YTD	Avg Volume	Previous Closing Price
HYG	iShares iBoxx $ High Yield Corporate Bond ETF	$17,949,331	11.71%	20,392,080	$87.47
JNK	SPDR Barclays High Yield Bond ETF	$10,268,319	13.52%	7,054,917	$109.15
BKLN	Invesco Senior Loan ETF	$4,836,277	8.01%	5,319,952	$22.76
HYLB	Xtrackers USD High Yield Corporate Bond ETF	$3,298,819	11.80%	561,683	$50.31
SJNK	SPDR Barclays Capital Short Term High Yield Bond E'	$3,264,710	8.13%	2,190,332	$27.10
SHYG	iShares 0-5 Year High Yield Corporate Bond ETF	$3,146,001	8.41%	518,505	$46.61

(Source: ETFDB, https://etfdb.com/etfdb-category/high-yield-bonds/)

If this book is correct and we enter into the biggest bond market drop in history, brought on by a strong dollar and high interest rates in a free market, politicians will be begging the banks to help bail *the politicians* out. The irony will be dramatic.

If you are short long-term junk bonds, or emerging market sovereign debt, you will be golden. Be on the alert, however, because it may be at this moment you should reasonably expect collaboration between the banks and government to emerge from the rubble of disaster, with some form of new digital currency announcement. This digital currency will be backed by, and/or run by, the banks and Federal Reserve (or successor entity) on behalf of governments. They may even task the NSA with getting in on the act:

NSA Working to Develop Quantum-Resistant Cryptocurrency: Report

"The United States' National Security Agency (NSA) is allegedly working to develop a quantum-resistant cryptocurrency. The claim was made in a tweet by Bloomberg Technology reporter William Turton on Sept. 4, who was in attendance at the Billington CyberSecurity 10th annual summit in Washington D.C.

'Anne Neuberger, Director of NSA's new Cybersecurity Directorate says that the agency will propose hardware and software standards again. Also notes agency is working to build quantum resistant crypto.'" (Source: Cointelegraph.com, https://cointelegraph.com/news/nsa-working-to-develop-quantum-resistant-cryptocurrency-report, by Marie Huillet, September 5, 2019).

For traders, this book recommends shorting long-term junk/high yield bonds and certain sovereign bonds, immediately. U.S. Government and other corporate long-term bonds should be shorted late in the fall of 2019, or early winter by January 15, 2020.

Especially regarding emerging-market long-term bonds, sell short as many as you can find, and pick those bonds with unfavorable or lower credit ratings. These debt issuances will get smashed in price in the years ahead. There are thousands of bonds in the market. Ask your broker to query junk bonds and see what he/she comes back with.

Fortunes will be made on short sales of corporate junk bonds and emerging market debt which needs to be paid back in dollars.

While U.S. treasury bonds may remain artificially "pegged" at a lower level by the Fed, the Fed cannot control the broad after-market in U.S. Treasury securities, or the overall yield curve in the U.S. and other nations. It also cannot control the interest rates demanded on the debt of overleveraged corporations. Take advantage of this impending crisis. The writing is on the wall, especially for junk bonds and emerging market sovereign debt.

Sell Short US Treasuries & Long-Term Bonds

Symbol	Name	Price 9/16/19	Yield	Date to Sell Short/Liquidate
ZB.U19	U.S. 30-Year Treasury Future	158 30^	2.30%	Sell short and/or liquidate all
ZN.U19	U.S. 10-Year Treasury Future	129 02^	1.84%	long-term bonds January 15,

Sell short any long-term corporate debt. Interest rate spikes will crush the value of these securities---especially junk bonds and ETF dividend/interest rate investments.

Short-term blue chip corporate paper will be more secure than government securities after 2023.

2020. Bonds likely to rally hard the fall of 2019; but interest rates expected to explode upward 2020-2024--- causing price collapse! Government attempts to "peg" rates will not be effective.

As a result, this book also recommends shorting long-term U.S. Treasury securities, accordingly; the longer the term, the better. Rates are expected to go through the roof on long-term debt, thereby crushing bond prices. The Fed will be caught between a decision of allowing runaway inflation by monetizing the debt, or allowing rates to rise. Ultimately, the Fed will blame the markets, even though the Fed caused the trouble in the first place, thereby "allowing" its Fed rate to rise. The reality is the market dictates all.

EPIC EMERGING MARKET DEBT & CURRENCY TRADE

The best highly-liquid trades may be to short the bonds of Brazil, the European Union, Japan and the emerging markets (and their currencies against the U.S. Dollar).

While the EU and Japan are not "emerging markets," they have been poorly run. Financial skeletons will come out of the closet over the course of the next several years for these countries. There are many other possible "shorts," and sophisticated traders who know how to short the Turkish Lira, certain Asian currencies, as well as other emerging market debt and currencies, versus a rising dollar, should ride the wave. The dollar will be super strong in a rising-rate environment.

An ETF with emerging-market bonds which may be an excellent short sale is: **VanEck Vectors J.P. Morgan EM Local Currency Bond ETF, Symbol: EMLC Recommendation: Timing Immediate** (Price 9/19/2019 $33.30)
Source: (ETFDB, https://etfdb.com/etf/EMB/#holdings)

Emerging Market Bond ETF
September 19, 2019

Symbol: EMLC		ETF Name: VanEck Vectors J.P. Morgan EM Local Currency Bond ETF*	
Holding	Weighting	Holding	Weighting
BRAZIL, FEDERATIVE REPUBLIC OF (GOVERNMENT)	1.88%	SOUTH AFRICA, REPUBLIC OF (GOVERN	1.14%
URUGUAY, ORIENTAL REPUBLIC OF (GOVERNMENT)	1.56%	MEXICO (UNITED MEXICAN STATES) (GC	1.07%
DOMINICAN REPUBLIC (GOVERNMENT)	1.54%	BRAZIL, FEDERATIVE REPUBLIC OF (GO\	1.04%
BRAZIL, FEDERATIVE REPUBLIC OF (GOVERNMENT)	1.45%	SOUTH AFRICA, REPUBLIC OF (GOVERN	1.03%
BRAZIL, FEDERATIVE REPUBLIC OF (GOVERNMENT)	1.43%	MEXICO (UNITED MEXICAN STATES) (GOVE	1.01%
PHILIPPINES, REPUBLIC OF THE (GOVERNMENT)	1.42%	PHILIPPINES, REPUBLIC OF THE (GOVERNM	0.97%
BRAZIL, FEDERATIVE REPUBLIC OF (GOVERNMENT)	1.17%	URUGUAY, ORIENTAL REPUBLIC OF (GOVEF	0.96%
DOMINICAN REPUBLIC (GOVERNMENT)	1.14%	* 266 Holdings in total.	

Readers are encouraged to explore "Emerging Markets Bond ETFs" via your search engine for other opportunities. The above ETF is among the most liquid for this sector. According to its holdings page, this fund has over 250 different securities in its portfolio.
"Selling short" long-term bonds of both corporate junk issuance (there are thousands of possible securities to choose from) and emerging market, or highly leveraged government sovereign debt, should be among the best trades. This strategy and recommendation is only for advanced investors and traders.

When prices drop due to sudden rate increases, investors panic and the floor falls out from underneath price support. Savvy investors who were short the Argentine Peso versus the U.S. Dollar know how this works. Literally, overnight, a currency (or sovereign debt issuance) can drop enormously.

The kind of panic the author is expecting in the emerging markets and among poorly-run sovereign states and companies is expected to be epic in the 2020s.

For super-aggressive investors/traders who want to stick to the U.S. markets, long-term put options would also be recommended (with put purchase no later than January 15, 2020 for expiration 1-2 years out) on five-, ten- and thirty-year U.S. Treasury Bonds; the longer the term, the likely the better the short.

Regardless, implement the sale of short positions in long-term bonds no later than January 15, 2020. Important: it is possible rates will drop into the fall of 2019. Use this as an opportunity to sell short at higher prices. Cover these short sales no later than December 31, 2023. Use a 10% trailing stop to keep yourself out of trouble (as you should be using stops for any trading positions). Rates may continue to rise into 2024, and you may leave great profit on the table by exiting at the end of 2023; however, the systemic risk brought on with increasing interest rates could cause a complete collapse of the securities industry. It won't matter if you have a gazillion dollars in theoretical profit if you can't get your money.

Also, don't be fooled by the moronic investors in Europe who are investing monies in securities yielding negative returns due to negative interest rates being offered at the banks and EU/Government levels. The politicians in the EU are desperate to make debt payments and keep markets calm. This is the reason they are desperately trying to artificially hold interest rates down.

Their actions will prove to be as futile as trying to hold off Mount Vesuvius eruptions. The outgoing President of the EU's Central Bank, Mario Draghi, will go down as the worst in history.

Like a cork driven from a shaken-up bottle of champagne, the EU is in for a disastrous ending to their debt party and quantitative easing experiments. Japan is in the same boat, as that government has also chosen to support every bond and stock in sight by having the government purchase them.

The "land of the rising sun" will likely be renamed the "land of the setting sun."

The sheer idiocy of allowing misguided spending, enormous debt and governing by perennial deficit by nearly all major countries on earth, has destroyed and encumbered the future of many generations of people. This could only have been done by career politicians who were paid off by the banking system.

A complete collapse of confidence will occur across emerging markets and Europe, creating an enormous rush to United States assets in both stocks and bonds in the early 2020s, especially. Because yields are at historic lows in bonds, most of the next round of capital investment will be seen in large, liquid stocks of successful U.S. companies.

In combination with a potential socialist grab for power in 2024 in the U.S. elections, rising rates will cause a serious debacle in the financial markets. The crashing sound of stocks falling from the threat of increasing taxes and hostility by the general population toward the players in the financial markets will be something to behold. Rates will be rising fast---they will make your head spin.

Fortunes are made and lost at moments like this. No fortunes will be made, however, by the "I drank the Kool-Aid" crowd on Wall Street. Those who do what their brokers tell them are doomed (e.g. "Just dollar cost average and buy some more...").

If you listen to the market speaking to us today, each sector is playing out an orchestration where the astute investor can prosper enormously in the difficult times ahead. You just have to listen to the music, carefully.

You will then know whether to be long, short, or have your assets in hand. This book may be invaluable in the effort to discern when and where the wild gyrations in the financial markets are expected to occur, and allow you to take action accordingly.

If things go according to plan, you should close all short bond positions and go to cash no later than December 31, 2023. Beginning at that time, do not allow any bank or broker to hold your assets in their possession. Make sure you have a private storage capability for precious metals, stock and bond certificates, as well as other tangible assets.

It is sage advice to start becoming extremely liquid and safe by the end of 2023.

There is a strong chance the "big rally," the greatest bull run in history, will continue into May of 2024 but, for purposes of this book and those reading it, get out at the end of 2023.

People in tune with the markets may choose to ride out the last part of the rally, as it could be quite amazing, but it will also be fraught with very high risk.

CHAPTER 8

FOREIGN EXCHANGE MARKETS

Many corporations will lose hundreds of millions of dollars in the coming years because they have not successfully hedged, or eliminated, their foreign exchange exposure properly. For multinational corporations this mistake will prove disastrous.

The might of the U.S. Dollar will be relentless in the coming years; the fall of 2019 may see some weakness in the dollar versus other currencies, however the world has little choice. Longer term the dollar will fly like Superman.

Despite the rampant whispering about replacing the U.S. Dollar and the "demise" of the U.S. Dollar, the pundits have conveniently forgotten two things:

1) The world is awash in debt denominated in U.S. Dollars. All of these debts must be repaid and thereby cause a tremendous, continued demand for U.S. Dollars. This will continue over the next several years.

2) The world's global derivatives trade, which dwarfs all nations' GDPs---is nearly all denominated in U.S. Dollars (as documented in <u>D'Apocalypse Now!</u>). The size of the derivatives market is estimated between $1½ - $2 Quadrillion Dollars. The total U.S. GDP is currently only approximately $21 Trillion and total *world* GDP is projected to be $88 Trillion in 2019.

Think about this for a minute. One Quadrillion is 1,000 Trillion. For the world's GDP to be on an equal par with derivatives, the world needs to create 75-100 economies the size of the United States.

As the good folk say…*"This just ain't gonna happen."*

Derivatives and the dangers of default throughout the system are documented to the extreme in <u>D'Apocalypse Now!</u> If you want to know more about this grave danger you should read that book ASAP.

Because of these two main reasons, the instructions for currencies are simple: Go long the U.S. Dollar and short everything else.

Especially vulnerable are the currencies from the emerging markets, the warning signs are all there.

We have already seen dramatic blow ups in the Turkish Lira, Argentinian Peso and many other currencies. Unending pressure has also been seen on the British Pound and the euro vis-à-vis the U.S. Dollar. Interestingly, shorting the Turkish Lira against the U.S. Dollar was a key position in the theoretical trading exercise carried out by Mr. Kelly from March 26-June 24, 2019, as discussed previously. It was a major contributor to the +124% performance.

Another key forecast previously made by the author was shorting the euro when it was at $1.3733/US Dollar on February 19, 2014 (the <u>D'Apocalypse Now!</u> publication date). Currency traders and travelers to Europe may remember the euro proceeded to tank, falling down to $1.0459/US Dollar by March 16, 2015. It then rebounded, and as this book goes to print, the euro is trading at approximately $1.0940/US Dollar.

Demacrash!

For readers who are not familiar with foreign exchange, a short sale of the euro executed at $1.40, with a drop down to $1.05, using an investment of $1 Million and 30:1 leverage, would have yielded a profit of $10,500,000. Many currency traders use much greater leverage and would have made even more money on this trade if they had followed the advice of Mr. Kelly in D'Apocalypse Now!

Because of the weak equity market expected for the fall of 2019, it is likely when the market tanks, the Fed will use quantitative easing and lower interest rates to fight back. Initially, this won't have an impact and the dollar will likely rise due to panic in the markets.

However, sooner or later, the dollar will likely pull back in a correction. This would be the safest period to initiate short sales of foreign exchange positions vs. the dollar, as outlined in this chapter.

For purposes of this book, January 2020 is the time to initiate new short sale positions in the euro, the British Pound, the Turkish Lira, Brazilian Real, the Mexican Peso, and the Japanese Yen. These currencies should be weak against the dollar for several years.

To date, the Japanese Yen has been a stalwart of strength versus the dollar when compared to many other currencies; however, the Japanese Yen is highly vulnerable. It may be one of the best shorts among the major currencies, because it hasn't dropped like the euro, the Peso, the Real and the British Pound the last couple of years. Look for the Yen to drop like a rock after the U.S. and China complete their trade deal. Even if the Yen continues to levitate magically, and trade talks drag on until after elections in 2020, the reward for shorting the Yen against the dollar will be big, very big.

Japan has some serious debt and fiscal-spending problems. The government has bought up virtually most of the bonds in every financing, while engaging in the outright purchase of many individual stocks. Tokyo bureaucrats made these decisions to provide near-term stability and enhance their political re-election aspirations. They believe by supporting markets they allow existing government to remain in power. Unfortunately, cost-push inflation around the world from inflated asset prices has caused economies to turn south. Decades of government easy-money policies are trembling earth itself, and the coming economic earthquake will shake the confidence in the Yen to its core but, the demise of the euro, for the same reasons, will happen much more quickly.

Provided Great Britain breaks away from the European Markets completely, shorting the euro vs. the dollar is looking quite good. In the following table, allocations to sell short the following foreign currencies vis-à-vis the U.S. Dollar are recommended as follows:

British Pound/US Dollar	5%
Euro/US Dollar	20%
US Dollar/Turkish Lira	20%
US Dollar/Mexican Peso	10%
US Dollar /Japanese Yen	25%
US Dollar/Brazilian Real	20%

Go Long the US Dollar

FX Pair	Name	Price 9/16/19 Sell Short	Go Long	Date to Sell Short/Go Long
EUR/USD	Euro/US Dollar	109.999		These currencies pairs
GBP/USD	British Pound/US Dollar	124.2		selected to take advantage
USD/TRY	US Dollar/Turkish Lira		5.7187	of a strong U.S. Dollar
USD/MXN	US Dollar/Mexican Peso		19.4318	Rising interest rates will
USD/JPY	US Dollar/Japanese Yen		108	crush other other currencies
USD/BRL	US Dollar/Brazilian Real		4.0835	vis-à-vis the U.S. "Greenback."
				Take positions on, or before, January 15, 2020.

Again, timing is everything in foreign exchange. The moves we will witness over the course of the period through 2024 will blow every trader's mind, or nearly so. **Go long or go short the positions in the "Go Long the US Dollar" table by January 15, 2020---and cover or close all positions, going to cash, by December 31, 2023.**

Demacrash!

There are going to be huge dollar moves, and because of the leverage involved with trading FX (i.e. Foreign Exchange), fortunes will be made and lost if you are on the right side, or the wrong side of a trade. Like anything else with leverage this is an advanced investors and traders game. It is not for people who are inexperienced trading FX.

The information in this chapter may be critical for corporations who maintain extensive international operations, whose true expertise is in producing and selling their products and services. They are not typically experts in foreign exchange.

Companies should be very leery of Mr. Goldman Sachs, and his brothers and sisters, structuring their trades. It may be best to seek independent advice from an entity not involved with the sale or purchase of a targeted swap, or transaction, prior to initiating a trade, or hedge. As the world has seen with Goldman Sachs, they can take both sides of a trade, and you may never know where you stand with them.

Strap on your helmet, because these currency markets will play havoc with corporations, central banks and traders, worldwide and they won't understand "why?" markets began moving much more violently than ever before.

If you are trading and not hedging, be aware: the volatility will be enormous. Stop-loss levels must be kept, but if you are in on a move early and catch the trade breaking your way, use very wide stops perhaps even as much as 15%, given expected high volatility.

Many FX dealers and brokerage firms will be emasculated in this wild arena the next few years. They will create very vicious counter-trend price moves to recoup losses when they bet against the dollar. Their panic can cause traders playing the long trend of a bullish dollar trade to become decidedly uncomfortable if the underlying bullish dollar position is initiated at an unfavorable opening price.

Demacrash!

With interest rates expected to rise dramatically (i.e. from 2020-2024), the U.S. Dollar will be KING. It will blow everyone away in fact, because most analysts today believe there is a raging bear market just waiting for the mighty greenback.

The flight to geopolitical safety is a once-in-a-lifetime event for most people, but the really "smart" guys at Goldman and Morgan don't even have this particular global, black-swan risk event on their radar screens. When the dollar becomes the bull in the china shop, all they will be able to do is repeat what Gomer Pyle would say:

"Surprise, Surprise!"

The "World's Most Fragile States" map published previously in Chapter 1 (page 17) visually portrays the "flight to safety" of capital the author expects to occur. This mapping of the flow of capital is laid over the map (see arrows and $ signs). After reading this chapter and then looking again on the map at the number of countries in weak positions currently, you can imagine what will happen to demand for the U.S. Dollar when that world map begins to collapse and "green" nations turn orange, and even red (FYI, in "black and white" print, this is difficult to see, but you can see darker and lighter shades on the map. The U.S. is strongest).

Forewarned is forearmed.

Similar to equities, as the markets approach 2024, risks increase. Ultimately, the dollar will collapse, but not before an apocryphal run. Regardless, the currency positions in this book for being long the U.S. Dollar versus other currency pairs should be closed prior to December 31, 2023. Given the markets expected volatility on all fronts, if you become dissatisfied with your "I drank the Kool-Aid" investment bank, do not be a deer caught in headlights. Make sure you take action. Your capital will depend on it, as the contagion will be ominous by the mid-2020s.

Chapter 9

2025+

Given the markets expected volatility on all fronts, if you become dissatisfied with your "I drank the Kool-Aid" investment bank, do not be a deer caught in headlights. Make sure you take action. Your capital will depend on it, and many lives around you may be affected. The contagion will be ominous by the mid-2020s.

As the three books in the <u>Federal Reserve Trilogy</u> have documented in detail, blame for the global economic meltdown in the last half of the 2020's can be left directly at the feet of the Federal Reserve and their cohorts in London, Paris and Germany, with great assists from debt-loving governments, worldwide.

The Fed's actions, supported by the U.S. Congress (both houses) and other governmental representatives in other countries, will cause a debt and derivatives collapse of monumental proportions. This was coined "D'Apocalypse" by the author.

Because of the mountain of debt, the Fed in collusion with politicians has kept the nectar of low interest rates available to governments for decades. As a result, politicians have cheated pensioners out of their incomes and forced thousands of money managers into high-risk investments. Along the way, they also created massive asset inflation, which has caused costs to soar, worldwide.

The numbers are universally galactic in size. The only way for governments to solve the problem is to either inflate their way out of it by printing *more* money, or allow massive economic contraction to take place. This would cause widespread bankruptcy for corporations, governments, and individuals alike.

When the global monetary meltdown hits, be on the lookout for a new digital currency to emerge. "Old" money may be declared illegal and forcibly exchanged for a fraction of its previous value. Alternatively, similar to what happened in Cyprus, your capital may merely be seized to pay for the banking industry's misdeeds.

Because people will lose all confidence in government, the outlook for precious metals is bright. Even if gold has one more severe sell-off below $1000/ounce, this sell-off will be the final set up for a rocket-ship ride which will set your hair on fire. Silver will ride the tide with gold and may be even more explosive to the upside.

For individuals in the U.S. the author recommends numismatic coins and either U.S. Buffalo Head one-ounce gold coins, or Canadian Maple Leaf one-ounce coins. They also are both 99% pure gold. Other coins of similar purity include, but are not limited to, the Chinese Panda and the Austrian Vienna Philharmonic. They aren't as well known in North America, however.

Silver coins from the U.S. Mint are also favored. The U.S. Silver Eagle coins might be easier to use in a crisis (i.e. it would be easier to fill up a gas tank with a silver one-ounce coin, perhaps worth $200/ounce, than a $5,000 gold coin).

Finally, to avoid seizure, or a declaration by government that owning gold coins is illegal, put half of your gold and silver coinage into the collectible/numismatic varieties with good grades. It is less likely government will outlaw an old coin, versus a new one.

Buy precious metals in coin or bar form *before* a crisis hits. The odds of purchasing a counterfeit gold/silver coin or bar, rises parabolically in an inflationary collapse situation.

In New York, the author can say Stack's Coins at 123 West 57th Street has been around a long time and might be a source for purchasing coins. The author has no affiliation, or relationship with Stack's, but personally would rather buy from a known brick-and-mortar source, than from an online operation (and the author is a "tech guy").

The reason for this is because of the rise in the quality of counterfeit coins and bars being sold into the marketplace. Given the mastery over the ability to create counterfeit coins and bars with nearly identical atomic weights---which look exactly like the real deal---it would be wise to purchase from a source which has a decade's long reputation to defend. You will pay a higher commission, no doubt.

As part of a family-run business, Stack's or other operations similar to it, are more likely to professionally inspect every coin and bar they receive. At a minimum, if you encounter fraud, you have a source with a reputation to turn to when you attempt to exchange your bad coins/bars for good ones. Make sure you keep your receipts, and ensure you photograph your purchase in the shop (with the receipt) which shows the year and appearance/grade of the coin or bar you purchased.

During the latter 2020's, governments worldwide will be on a massive hunt for taxes, as they already are. There will be bank failures, brokerage failures and bankruptcies. Any money or securities you have in a bank, or securities firm, will be at risk.

The state credit ratings you see, as follows, are likely not worth much because they are in reality likely much, much worse than published. Those who remember the financial crisis know full well the ratings agencies are organizations with a massive conflict of interest. They get paid by their customer to provide that customer with a rating which would allow the customer to sell bonds, or other securities to the public.

This fraudulent set up will once again blow up in the face of investors and the ratings agencies. The author, for the record, recommends no state, local or federal government obligations of *any kind* be purchased. ZIPPO. NADA. NOTHING!

State Credit Ratings by Moody's Investors Service
March 1, 2019

Illinois Credit Rating Lowest In Nation---One Notch From Junk

	Investment Grade
Aaa	Delaware, Georgia, Indiana, Iowa, Maryland, Missouri, North Carolina, South Carolina, South Dakota, Tennessee, Texas, Utah, Vermont, Virginia
Aa1	Alabama, Arkansas, Colorado, Florida, Hawaii, Idaho, Massachusetts, Michigan, Minnesota, Montana, Nebraska, New Mexico, New Hampshire, North Dakota, New York, Ohio, Oregon, Washington, Wisconsin
Aa2	Arizona, Kansas, Maine, Mississippi, Nevada, Oklahoma, Rhode Island, West Virginia
A1	Connecticut
A2	
A3	New Jersey
Baa1	
Baa2	
Baa3	Illinois

	Speculative Grade "Junk"
Ba1	...(9 Additional Junk Ratings)
C	

Source: Moody's Investors Service
Note: Wyoming is not rated by Moody's Investor Service
Credit: WIREPOINTS

144

Demacrash!

If you must own debt in an era of rising interest rates, only purchase from blue chip companies with top-rated commercial paper and a term of less than one year. If you buy any government securities, purchase U.S. Treasury Bills, less than one year and buy them directly from the government.

The next crisis, like the last one, will be about capital protection, not comparing interest rates at banks and praying the FDIC will back you up. Those actions will be a fool's errand.

To hammer it home: the blow up will be primarily due to derivatives and counter-party risk in direct combination with wasteful spending and outright egregious benefit-grabbing by the bureaucracy (both elected and unelected). The entire Western financial system will be shaken to the ground.

Your bank in Sleepytown, USA may have done nothing wrong, but its inter-banking activities with larger banks may cause it to be indirectly and significantly involved with derivatives transactions. This causes risk to rise dramatically for the unsuspecting investor and depositor. Check your local bank and see what correspondent banks they deal with. If they are the big banks, you know you may surely have trouble in the future. Weiss ratings online may also provide you with a good screening tool for banks: https://weissratings.com/.

Once again, to the extent you can, physically hold your securities certificates personally and carry nothing in "street name." Place significant amounts of cash and other valuables in a private storage vault beginning in 2024, at the latest. Many secured private vaults are available and there are some good ones in Canada.

Corporations should close all derivatives positions by the end of 2023. Making this decision will cause a short-term hit to earnings, but will likely save the company. Make *sure* all securities and assets are stored privately.

This coming debt apocalypse will present a situation where you will be glad you have a plan to guarantee the return of your principal, while hedging against inflationary spirals due to shortages, or outright destruction of currencies through the monetization of debt.

Like a Sine or Cosine wave, sector inflation will rise dramatically and then collapse in a debt-driven deflationary spiral. This will very likely bring on a "new" currency which forcibly exchanges "old" currency units for "new" ones at unfavorable exchange rates. People may lose the value of 50% or more of their money overnight. This scenario already happened in Cyprus. A few oligarchs got bailed out in front of the pack, but the rest of the people had their money stolen from them. The dominoes will likely fall in Europe first, then Asia, or parts thereof, and then the U.S. They are already fallen in most of South America.

The difference this time is the new currency will be digital. You will be forced to use it and exchange your existing dollars, euros, pounds, etc. for the new monetary system's currency. There will be no escaping the slaughter of your wealth unless you have converted your wealth into tangible assets which continue to hold relative value. Money in a bank account will be wiped out, and your securities firm may seize your funds.

ADVENT OF WAR?
The U.S. will benefit in the next few years, as its safe-haven status provides liquidity for big money. As the years progress and interest rates take their toll on budget expenses and economic growth, politicians will kill to stay in power as the economy slips away.

If we look at history, we know wars start in times of economic distress and turmoil. And globally, even today, turmoil prevails.

Remembering an historic trick politicians have used to stay in office, may be of importance and provide insight. They discovered, long ago, if people start thinking about a "patriotic" effort, rather than an economic catastrophe, they stand a better chance for reelection. This often means starting a war and blaming someone else for it.

Bankers love war because this means governments borrow more money, and bankers prefer debt backed by taxpayer dollars. The impact of war on regular people is far less ideal. World War II families have shared many stories of food shortages and basic necessities, while recounting even worse stories about their grandparents' (or parents') Great Depression experience in the 1930s. Of course, these sacrifices pale in comparison with the millions of deaths caused by war itself.

Today, these lessons are forgotten by most people. This is why we are destined to repeat the mistakes of history. The experience may not be identical, but it will rhyme. People will panic, hoard goods, and money will be nowhere to be found except among the elite.

Remember, the rules and regulations put in place by the Federal Reserve (and Congress) for the banks and investment banking firms have changed in favor of the banks. That cash you think is yours, or those securities you hold in your brokerage firm, are *not* yours. They are owned by the banks and brokerages, which can use your assets for collateral and to meet obligations, especially in a crisis.

If you don't believe this, you need look no further than the closing of MF Global, once one of the world's largest commodity firms, and the actions of its CEO, Jon Corzine (former CEO of Goldman Sachs and Governor of New Jersey). This firm took hundreds of millions of dollars from client accounts at Corzine's direction, without permission from the customer when their business failed.

And, you guessed it…nobody went to jail.

The banks can and will prevent you from accessing your assets. You, whether an individual or company, merely have standing as a lender to the bank, or investment bank/broker you work with.

Demacrash!

If you do not prepare for 2025[+], then you must be OK with getting in line with thousands of other people trying to gain access to capital. There will not be enough to go around. Do everything in your power to obtain your stock certificates and minimize the amount of cash in a bank, investment bank, or brokerage firm.

Bankers have historically been hung by angry crowds; this author's suspicion is we will see a repeat of this ugly behavior in the years ahead. Bankers, politicians and unelected bureaucrats, bloated with fat paychecks, may meet up with angry mobs and a society at large which scorns them, even more than they do today, if that is even possible.

"Let them eat cake," will simply not suffice. People will likely want heads to roll when the bottom falls out. This is completely wrong to want vengeance, but history tells us this is what may happen.

As the author provided counsel in <u>The Federal Reserve Trilogy</u>, the period ahead is one which provides an opportunity to reunite and bring you closer to those around you, while remembering and honoring the fact God is in charge. You can find peace, especially if you are a Christian, with the recognition all of these problems coming at us are necessary for the end times to arrive.

It is quite easy to see how a world-wide banking and governmental panic would set the stage for a global, digital currency. While many believe this is a far-fetched idea, and not credible, take a look at what Amazon just announced. Then think about the many adaptations of digital currencies in the world, today. Are we being prepped?

Is this "the" setup for a one-world currency transaction system discussed in this book, or as prophesied in <u>The Bible</u>?

Amazon tests Whole Foods payment system that uses hands as ID

"Forget the titanium Apple Card — Amazon's latest payment method uses flesh and blood. The e-tailing giant's engineers are quietly testing scanners that can identify an individual human hand as a way to ring up a store purchase, with the goal of rolling them out at its Whole Foods supermarket chain in the coming months, The Post has learned...The high-tech sensors are different from fingerprint scanners found on devices like the iPhone and don't require users to physically touch their hands to the scanning surface." (Source: New York Post, September 3, 2019, by Nicolas Vega).

History, once again, is a good teacher. The book of Revelation, from history's oldest printed book written 2,000 years ago says:

The Mark of the Beast

"[16]It also forced all people, great and small, rich and poor, free and slave, to receive a mark on their right hands or on their foreheads,[17]so that they could not buy or sell unless they had the mark, which is the name of the beast or the number of its name.

[18]This calls for wisdom. Let the person who has insight calculate the number of the beast, for it is the number of a man. That number is 666." (Source: The Bible, Revelation 13:16-19, New International Version).

What might this mean today? Could someone from the time of Jesus, like the Apostle John who wrote the Book of Revelation, have had a vision of transactions in the future which required approval, by the reading of a "mark" on the face, or hand?

The fact is today, facial recognition software and Artificial Intelligence make it possible to look at "marks" on the face, or hands, and digitally link you to a database (which could easily include your credit card and bank account). From there it is child's play from a software perspective, to execute a transaction.

In a vision of the future from 2,000 years ago on the island of Patmos, the Apostle John may very well have been watching modern technology he saw, but may not have fully understood. The "marks" he described may even be unique to each person. Today, thanks to DNA, we know everyone has unique "marks." DNA fundamentally shapes unique lines and traces on our faces and hands, easily allowing modern technology to "read" them.

Are these the "marks" seen by John?

The Book of Revelation, in light of the dramatic news by Amazon, is a must read. Amazon, as clear as day, has an invention which fulfills John's prophecy 2,000 years ago from a practical technology perspective.

As more signs emerge---"D'Apocalypse" market crashes, earthquakes, fires, tsunamis, hurricanes, wars, the emergence of evil, etc. perhaps it might be time to really read the Book of Revelation, every page, and ask if its pages speak to you. Are nations aligning against one another? Are earthquakes happening with greater frequency? Are there wars and rumors of wars? Are Principalities and Powers battling away? Revelation's poetic imagery allows each and every one of us to decide if Jesus is the son of God.

For the author, the evidence piled up is overwhelming, and the verdict is in. Jesus Christ is the son of God and He came to forgive our sins. Belief in Him gives us eternal life. Alleluia!

It is with great hope the readings and knowledge contained in this book helps you and your family in the years ahead. Good luck, good investing, and God bless you and yours.

Author's Personal Note

Invitation to Make a Commitment

Demacrash! is a work of financial forecasting. While Jackass Banker and the author believe it may be correct in its predictions, the world knows it is impossible to be correct all the time. There often are big "whiffs" (also known as "strike-outs") when trying to make predictions, especially concerning the financial markets.

Nevertheless, Mr. Kelly believes there is evil approaching for the markets and wants people to be ready. Hopefully, many readers will prosper and be in a position to help others in the trying years ahead.

The foundation for Demacrash! is built upon Mr. Kelly's investigative, exhaustive work with The Federal Reserve Trilogy. The Trilogy's books include The $30 Trillion Heist---The Federal Reserve---Scene Of The Crime?, The $30 Trillion Heist---The Federal Reserve---Follow The Money! and D'Apocalypse™ Now!---The Doomsday Cycle.

Together, they prove vital to discovering the truth of what bankers did to America during the credit crisis from 2007-2010. These books also will help readers become prepared for the dangers heading our way, both societally and economically.

The forecasts made were profound and became eerily accurate by 2017. The predictions included:

1) The Dow Jones Industrial average reaching 22,000 – 37,000;

2) The euro collapsing from $1.3733 (it hit a low of $1.0459, so far); and

3) The price of gold dropping from near $1,500 in 2013 (when the book was written) to at least $1,156.86. Gold ultimately dropped to $1,069.20/ounce, before bouncing and triggering buy signals, laid out specifically in D'Apocalypse Now!

Without a proper understanding of the Federal Reserve, readers will find it difficult to understand why America has changed dramatically in seemingly dastardly ways, at all points of the compass. It is only through the process of education can reform get accomplished.

Understanding the fact the Federal Reserve is *the problem* is critical to the reader's ability to educate Congressmen, Senators, neighbors and friends. As you try to educate, be aware some don't want to be educated and are benefactors of the Fed's egregious actions against the masses.

If you don't know Jesus Christ and you are led by the Holy Spirit, pray to Jesus for your salvation and watch the miracle of a changed life begin to take place. You will no longer fear for the future, but will find you are now in the army of God and are one of His confident foot soldiers who *knows* they will be victorious in the end.

It is the best retirement plan.

God bless you. He is mighty, indeed!

FOREVER CHANGE YOUR LIFE

"Dear God, the sole God for all eternity, I pray in your son's name, Jesus Christ, to please forgive my sins and hear my prayer. I accept Jesus Christ as my Lord and personal savior and believe you sent Him from heaven to earth, where He was born of the Virgin Mary. I believe in His life, His teachings, His horrible death and the sacrifice He made for my sins---and all mankind's sins. I KNOW AND BELIEVE HIS RESURRECTION IS TRUE AND I KNOW AND BELIEVE HE ASCENDED INTO HEAVEN AND SITS AT THE RIGHT HAND OF THE FATHER. I accept your gift and promise of eternal life through faith in Jesus Christ, for you have promised us by your grace, the grace of the one and only eternal God, I can be saved through the gift of faith. I also know my earthly works will not get me into your heavenly kingdom because you don't want any man to boast. I know we are created in Jesus to do good works out of the love and gratefulness we have for your mercy, power and gift of eternal life through the sacrifice made for us by Jesus Christ, your son and savior. AMEN"

"For it is by grace you have been saved, through faith—and this is not from yourselves, it is the gift of God—not by works, so that no one can boast. For we are God's handiwork, created in Christ Jesus to do good works, which God prepared in advance for us to do." (Source: The Bible, Ephesians 2:8-10, New International Version).

"For God so loved the world that He gave His only begotten son, that whosoever believeth in Him should not perish, but have eternal life." (Source: The Bible, John 3:16, King James Version).

If you pray this prayer, or a form of prayer accepting Jesus Christ as your Lord and Savior, I urge you to find brothers and sisters in Christ to nurture your walk with God. The Holy Spirit will guide you and you will notice a difference in the way you walk and talk through life...you will see differences in your attitudes and actions. Embrace these, read and study His Holy Word, The Bible, and *repent* of your sins. Your heart will naturally want to do good works, because you realize what an amazing *free* gift has been given to you---ETERNAL LIFE.

After all the reading, studying, successes, failures, sacrifices and opportunities in life---there is only one thing which matters.

Jesus.

Christian Cross in the Roman Coliseum

www.ingramcontent.com/pod-product-compliance
Lightning Source LLC
Chambersburg PA
CBHW030842210326
41521CB00025B/648